Find Where the Wind Goes

Moments from my life

Find Where the Wind Goes

Moments from my life

Second Edition

DR. MAE JEMISON

SIGNAL HILL ROAD PUBLISHING, LLC

Published by
SIGNAL HILL ROAD PUBLISHING, LLC

signalhillroad.com

ISBN-13: 978-1-63725-000-6

BIOGRAPHY & AUTOBIOGRAPHY
Adventurers & Explorers / Women / African American & Black
/ Science & Technology

YOUNG ADULT NONFICTION
Biography & Autobiography / Science & Technology / Women

Written by Mae Jemison, M.D.
Design and Layout by Jason D. Batt
Art by StudioNYC

Second Edition

DEDICATION

I wrote this book—a collection of moments from my life growing up, not really an autobiography—in response to a question I am
frequently asked, *"What advice would you give to my teenage son or
daughter who wants to ... ?"*

Firmly believing that example and experience arc the best teachers, the advice I would give to a teenager is very much the same that
I would give to a younger child or an adult. It is the same my mother
gave to me "Pay attention to and learn from all the adventures you
have in life, big and small, for within each there is a valuable insight
to help you throughout your life. And, when the lessons that originate from satisfying your curiosity, appear to conflict with maintain-
ing your dignity, they are particularly important. It seems to me that
these curiosity-dignity tension-filled events reach a peak when we
are teenagers, age-wise, or adolescents in terms of our experience in
a situation. We know quite a lot, but not so much to restrain us from
taking risks, pushing boundaries, or making mistakes from which we
rebound stronger, wiser, and more resilient."

These are my reflections on life events that I believe my 16-year-old self would have wanted to know. Though focused on young adults, I wrote this book for all of those who, like me, constantly have the answer to a life problem or direction right at their fingertips. While we may only manage to grab and hold onto a fragment, still we continue happily forward. I hope these stories and ideas are fun and enlightening for those young and old, girls and boys.

Here are moments when satisfying my curiosity seemed squarely at odds with my supposed dignity. So, I dedicate this book to the friends in my life who, with humor, always embodied the beautiful balance of dignified curiosity: Tiger, Pink, Gray, Pili, Mac, Lil' Mama, and Sneeze.

CONTENTS

WIND CURRENTS
Who I Intended To Be

"*What do you want to be when you grow up?*"
Looking around the room, I saw the magical board with the colorful felt sun, flowers, and trees that stuck without glue, and I thought, "I know the answer to that." I waved my hand excitedly, arm straight up in the air. I could barely hold my response inside while the teacher called on the other five and six year olds. They said *"fireman," "police officer," "mailman," "teacher," "mother."* I had my answer. It was none of these.

Finally, the teacher called on me. Without hesitation, I answered emphatically, *"I want to be a scientist."*

The teacher looked puzzled and slightly taken aback. I can't say I know exactly what was wrong with my answer. Perhaps as my teacher looked around the kindergarten at Mc-Cosh Elementary School, on the southside of inner-city Chicago, she was just surprised. Maybe she was thrown off by this skinny, brown-skinned girl with short hair, who despite her babysitter's best efforts, might come to school a bit disheveled. Though obviously quite bright—this girl could already read and knew all her numbers—she refused to act like a little lady on the way to school with her older brother and sister or anywhere else. Maybe the teacher felt it was her job to help her students set realistic goals. In 1961, becoming a scientist was not in the realm of possibility for most people—and certainly not for a little colored girl. (African Americans were still called and called ourselves "colored" back then.) So the teacher replied, *"Don't you mean a nurse?"*

To be honest, at that moment I did not worry about her thoughts. I was just plain indignant. She doubted me, as if I didn't know what a scientist was, or worse, that I was incapable of becoming one. I simply put my hands on my hips and said, *"No, I mean a scientist!"*

Years later, after I had earned a bachelor's degree in Chemical Engineering and was in medical school, I slipped and told a friend of a friend that I was going to apply to be an astronaut. He laughed loudly and said, *"You mean like the guys who go to the moon? Give me a break."*

Today, looking back at my life growing up and forward toward future possibilities, I'm struck by how the flow of life events is like the wind.

Events that change us and redirect our lives may begin very subtly, much like small changes in air temperature. There is a slight rustle of tree leaves, yet if one observes the accompanying signs, one can forecast the next day's weather. The hint of a breeze that kisses your cheek may turn into a full-fledged hurricane that uproots trees and old ideas. Wind can flood the shoreline and change the course of rivers. A miniscule drop in atmospheric pressure may signal a tornado that in one intense minute, knocks over buildings and demolishes blocks to the imagination. The next second, the wind is gone, but your path in life is altered forever.

Life stretches in front of and behind us, made up of the actions we and others took. I wonder: "Is it possible to see the trends?" The small stirring of air as I waved my hand back and forth in kindergarten created only a slight breeze. What became of that breeze?

What currents in my life began just then? Where did that wind lead?

My story, to date, is not a mystery. You may even know the ending, up to a point. I say "up to a point" because I am still alive. My life, I imagine and hope, continues to hold secrets, new challenges, varied opportunities, important lessons, good times and unforeseen directions.

My career has been in the physical sciences and technology, but also in the social sciences. I got through elementary school; the riots in the Chicago ghettos in the 1960s; short natural hair combined with puberty (whew!); integrated high schools, whether that cute football player liked me as much as I liked him; chemical engineering at Stanford University in California and medical school at Cornell University in New York City; Cambodian refugee camps; questioning whether my country loved me as much as I was supposed to love it; the reality of being a doctor in West Africa; adjusting to summers in Houston, Texas—well, just Texas, period; astronaut training, military pilots, and spaceflight; learning about death; relinquishing the dream to be a fashion designer, an architect, and professional dancer; crushes on famous, fictional, and not-so-famous men; and quasi-celebritydom. I went through all of that seeking to find where the wind goes. And I am still not sure.

I can say, however, that I have found there are always hints along the way; childhood is filled with them. Some I paid attention to, some I missed completely, and quite a few I just chose to ignore. This is a brief collection of some moments that taught me lessons and carried me aloft to this place, this day. I want to share some of my best clues, but I know there will definitely be more to come.

Because the currents continue throughout our lives to lead us to new discoveries.

WHISPERS ON THE WIND

DADDY, MOTHER, AND OTHER FOLKS

M ae Carol Jemison. I was born in October in Decatur, Alabama, the third child of Dorothy and Charlie
Jemison. It must have been on an auspicious day—why else
would I have chosen it? As you can imagine, I do not remember
much about the day. I am sure what I do remember is totally
confused with what my parents said, and what my brother and
sister brainwashed me to believe for their own sibling-inspired
purposes. In truth, I am not sure that anything I recall before
the age of two is more than a kind of "thought insertion."

I lived the first three and a half years of my life in Decatur,
a small town in northern Alabama that had a population of

approximately 30,000 in the late 1950s when I first arrived. I remember hot, sunny streets and, occasionally, torrential rains. I had to look up at everything! Decatur was not busy—you could walk in the middle of the street in front of our house— yet it was quite adequate for my purposes back then. I just needed a nice, sunny, warm place near relatives to spend the first few years of my life. Since I have been back as an adult, I realize Decatur would probably have been described as "sleepy." Decatur is adjacent to Huntsville, Alabama, location of the Red Stone Arsenal, home to the patriot missiles used in the Desert Storm Operation, and the Marshall Space Flight Center, where I would later spend many hours training as an astronaut.

The story goes that I was a cute baby. All the nurses called me "Rosebud" because of the shape of my lips. I was told that I was a very happy infant who smiled easily and did not cry much. As I grew into a toddler, my father nicknamed me "Fattening Bug." I loved that name because I was thrilled to be growing bigger.

I lived with my mother, Dorothy; my father, Charlie; my brother and sister, Ricky and Ada Sue, on one side of a two-family duplex owned by my mother. Mr. John and Miss Ada, my mother's adoptive parents, were from Florence, Alabama, where my mother, an only child, had grown up. Florence is also where my siblings were born. My paternal grandparents, Primus and Susie Jemison, lived in Talladega, Alabama, where my father and his older brother, my uncle Louis, grew up. Uncle Louis went to Talladega College, one of the oldest black universities in the country. My mother also went to Talladega College for a year. But they did not know each other and, no that's not where she met my father. They met at a dance. I believe Cab Calloway, the famous bandleader who made zoot suits popular, was performing. At least, that's where I arranged for them to meet.

Recalling people from when you're three years old, isn't really about facial features. I believe you actually identify the essence of a person's being. Perhaps it is a smell, an electrical field or aura, the sound of someone's voice, or someone's touch, but only the most obvious physical details are recorded.

I knew my mother; she was my mother. She was very smart, took care of me, and always kept me safe. As I grew older, I realized my mother was very pretty and had what black people back then called a "tempting tan." I don't know exactly what that meant, but it referred to skin color. My mother left college after two years to care for her ailing parents. For the first years of my life, she stayed at home, took care of us, worked occasional cleaning jobs, and sewed clothes to make extra money.

My father was tall, dark-skinned, sometimes stern and sometimes playful. I looked forward to him coming home every evening. He worked as a roofer, which meant he was up on ladders and roofs handling hot tar. My father always sported a mustache, beard, goatee, or some type of facial hair. I found out later he was considered a good-looking man, and his nickname was "Side Burns." We called him "Daddy" and we called my mother "Mother." Or as we pronounced it, "Mutha"—after all, we were in the South.

Some of my most vivid memories in Decatur center around food. Specifically, "Bee-bops." Known as freeze cups in the North, Bee-bops were sweet drinks frozen in paper cups. The sugar that settled and froze at the bottom was the best part. The "Bee-bop Lady" (I have no idea what her real name was) lived a few houses up the street and sold candies and cookies as well. We'd walk down the hot, sun-drenched Alabama street to her house. My bare feet burned on the scalding concrete. But once I purchased the Bee-bops with my few pennies, the pavement would no longer burn. The syrup would mix with water condensed on the cup and drip down my hand. My clothes were rapidly soiled. At that point, the only thing that could make me happier would be to tag along with my older brother and sister on one of their fantastic adventures—or maybe eating a Moon Pie.

Here are some facts about brothers and sisters. I am an adult now, and I should try to be fair to Ada Sue and Ricky, my sister and brother, also known as "the antagonists" in various chapters of my life and, truth be told, also frequently allies. I do know it is a drag for my older siblings to have a younger sibling like me stumbling along behind just because our parents said they had to take me along. Ha, ha! But that's life, and the price you have to pay for being older siblings. As the youngest child, you always desperately want to do whatever your older brother and sister do. You will capitulate to all types of indignities, cheating, mistreatment, mind control, and physical restraint, just to be allowed to tag along. And your older siblings know this.

So my very earliest memory was hard won. I turned and looked at the backrest of the chair I had been sitting in. It was covered in a light sky-blue, maybe satin brocade fabric. I saw bloodstains where my head had been. I had just experienced a well-known childhood trauma: being accidentally hit on the head with a rock thrown by a sibling or friend.

Another early memory centers around what enticed my "sibs" to play with me voluntarily. Ricky and Ada Sue liked to blow on my belly and tickle me until I couldn't breathe. I'd laugh so hard that I thought my belly and sides would never stop cramping and hurting. They would sneak in and do this when my mother wasn't looking. I was also a welcome diversion during the vesicular stage of my chicken pox. That's when watery blisters—or "vesicles" as I later learned they were called in medical school—could be burst open and scabs pulled off. I know you may think "Yuck!" But I have come to appreciate that "yuck" is precisely the job of siblings. Younger or older, siblings are around to introduce us to icky things, to teach us humility, enable us to cope with the elements of surprise and fear, and present us with challenges, like how to get into their rooms, clothes, and secrets, and how to keep them out of ours.

"Sibs" teach us the rewards of perseverance in competition: how to eat the fastest, how to hold off from doing the chores the longest (my personal best for not washing dishes was two days, which included innovative hiding places), how to pass the blame and make accusations stick (I never won, I would always laugh), and how to get the best treatment from parents, aunts and uncles, and other adult members of the extended family. I could also count on Ada Sue and Ricky to support me whether things were good or not. We may have had our personal skirmishes, but we always wanted the best for one another. We were proud of each other's accomplishments and would help each other with tasks (as long as it wasn't washing the dishes). The alliances between us shifted as we grew older—Ada Sue and Ricky versus Mae; Mae and Ada Sue versus

Ricky; Ricky and Mae versus Ada Sue; or everyone for himself or herself—but we've always been very close.

MY LIFE IN DECATUR: LEARNING THE ROPES

When I was two and three years old, I would begin my day with helping my mother get my six-year-old brother and seven-year-old sister ready for and off to school. As I walked with my mother to take Ada Sue and Ricky to Westlawn Elementary School, I always tried to maintain my balance along a curb that bordered a small pond. I imagined that small pond on my right had lily pads, frogs, and all sorts of other magical creatures in it. Later in the day, my mother and I might sew clothes, cook, or pay a nickel and take the bus downtown to go shopping. We would read stories together. I don't remember when I actually learned how to read. It seems I always knew my letters and sounds and numbers, and at least how to count to 100.

My absolute favorite thing to do was to go visit my Aunt Hannah. She was really my great-great aunt. Everyone was so surprised by how well Aunt Hannah and I got along, since Aunt Hannah was not known to "suffer fools kindly." In fact, she was noted for having a bit of a temper and was not necessarily an *"Oh, I just love children"* kind of woman. Yet, I remember sitting just as happily with her talking, solving the problems of the world, and learning. Everyone said that I was like Aunt Hannah. My mother would leave me there sometimes and I would cook with her. I am not quite sure where in Decatur she lived. We had to take the bus to get there or my father had to drive us in the car. Oh yeah, there's a story about the car.

My father had a Buick. He always drove Buicks. So I know that it was a Buick I wrecked when at two years old I first stretched my "*Let's explore*" and "*I can do that too*" wings.

My mother, my father, two of his friends, and I had gone shopping. My father pulled into the parking lot and my mother got out quickly to pick up some groceries. She found she needed help carrying the bags back, so my father got out to help her. He left the car running because he was only going to be a few minutes. It was the 1950s and gasoline prices and the environment were not issues yet.

Well, I decided I could drive and I jumped into the driver's seat. My father's friends didn't realize what I had planned. By some stroke of kid luck, determination, and mimicry, I depressed the clutch, put the car in gear, gave it a little gas, and got the car moving before anyone knew anything. Everything was just dandy with the mechanics of the getting-the-car-to-move part. However, the steering part—you know, looking over the wheel, turning it to make the car go one way or the other—was difficult. The level of difficulty was evident three dented cars later.

My adventure ended abruptly. Daddy was incredulous that I had gotten the car started and moving. Mother was trying to figure out how I had evaded two grown men and gotten behind the wheel in the first place. My parents were both thankful that nothing had happened to me. I thought I was pretty special and grinned broadly. I did not get a spanking or get yelled at. My father's friends … they're another story.

All this happened in Decatur, Alabama before I was four years old. I know because I celebrated my fourth birthday in Chicago on 61st Street and Ellis Avenue. There was caramel icing on a yellow cake with pink candles. Almost everyone was gathered around: Aunt Mary, Aunt Martha, Aunt Melvyn, Uncle Tootsie, my cousin Lenore, my brother and sister Ricky and Ada Sue, and my mother. But my father was not.

CHICAGO BOUND

We seemed to be standing in a dark cave. I don't remember if it was night or day. The warmth, humidity, and smell of diesel fuel was stifling. I had on a pretty little dress that I had not

managed to dirty yet. Trains rolled into the station. The train we stood next to seemed to be alive as it hissed steam. It was so big! I was not even as tall as the wheels! I could see all the gears, nuts, and bolts; it looked so complicated. The train and the idea of traveling to some new place fascinated me, though no one else seemed as excited. My mother, brother, sister, and I boarded a train in Decatur and went to Chicago, without my father.

My sister tells me that my mother was unhappy with the job opportunities in Alabama. My mother had completed two years of college, but still could only find work cleaning white people's houses. She had left college to care for her ill parents, and once she was married and had three children, she had little opportunity to complete her college degree in Alabama. We were part of the great migration of black people from the South to Northern cities, seeking economic opportunities and improvement of their lives.

In Chicago, though, my mother did complete college and then became a schoolteacher. She went on to get her master's degree and took up writing, as well.

I thought my father hadn't wanted to leave Alabama. He made me smile. Just like any other three-year-old who was taken care of by her mother, I wanted to be with mine. But I didn't know why my father couldn't be there, too. There seemed to be a hole in everything. I found out later that he had stayed to settle everything in Decatur.

Being little kids, once we arrived in Chicago, even under those circumstances, Ada Sue, Ricky, and I laughed and played, roughhoused really. We frequently played tag and "Purple People Eater," and once I fell off the bed onto the concrete floor of the basement apartment of my Aunt Mary and Uncle Tootsie's graystone. That's where my mother, brother, sister, and I lived. My head hit so hard I saw stars. I couldn't think. I couldn't breathe. I didn't know if I would live. I was just there. I caught my breath and then I cried and cried and cried and "swup-swupped." You know that noise little kids make when they try to stop crying, try to take a deep breath, and try to keep mucus from running down their nose with their lip quivering, all at the same time? "Swup-swupping." I cried some more and finally stopped "swup-swupping." Then it dawned on me, I was alive, still intact. *Hey, I'm kinda resilient.* My head was pretty hard after all. I could take a hard knock and still survive. The wind picked up speed.

Later that fall, just a bit after my fourth birthday, Ricky looked out the window and shouted, "There's Daddy!" My father had left Decatur and had come to Chicago to be with us. We had only been separated a couple of months, but months seem like a long time when you're a child. Now my father was here with us and we were happy. The family was all together.

We soon moved from my uncle and aunt's house into a dubious three-room apartment that we stayed in for only one or two months. We dubbed it "The Stink House," because the toilet in the lavatory shared with other tenants backed up too frequently for comfort. My father, not the landlord, would always fix it.

I started nursery school at that time because my mother worked. I was always so proud that my mother worked because back then most women did not. I thought she was very special. The station wagon picked me up from home to carry me to The Growing Years Nursery School. It arrived each morning before my brother and sister left for school. I was dropped back home after they returned from school. I guess we were what folks now call "latchkey" children, because we went to school and came back without our parents being home.

During the early 1960s things were a bit different from today. I'm not sure if there were fewer perils for children, but as kids we knew not to go outside when no adult was home. Rules which were not to be broken included not answering the door, not letting anyone else in the house whether we knew them or not, and not playing with fire. So, at four, seven, and eight years old, we did just fine for the two or three hours a day we were by ourselves.

One game we played was to peep out of the door and look for my mother. She usually would arrive home between 4:30 and 5 p.m. During one of those peeping games I was hit in the head by the doorknob, and a "great big ol' hickey" immediately jumped on my forehead. I cried a bit, "swup-swupped," but you know that passed quickly since I was already getting a well-deserved reputation for having a hard head.

STILL NOT QUITE A PHYSICIAN

I came face-to-face with the sorrow of death during our two-month-long stint in "The Stink House." There Peep-Peep, the Easter chick, met an untimely demise.

Practicing trampoline moves on the bed with wooden slats was not encouraged or even allowed, but, hey, it was fun. And let's just say that when I was jumping up and down on the mattress with the dear little chick, he did not jump out of the way with as much alacrity and skill as my four-year-old mind supposed he possessed. I noticed that he (I assumed that it was a "he" chick, but I did not know how to tell) was not making happy peep-peep sounds anymore after I stepped on him, and his head was lying limply to the side. I had accidentally broken Peep-Peep's neck. I was so scared. I felt so bad.

When I saw he was no longer jumping with me, I moved

quickly and decisively. I cracked the window. I knew that people needed more air when they were faint—maybe this would work for other animals, too. I put Peep-Peep in the cool air to revive him. It was March in Chicago and cold. I cried and cried because I couldn't believe the chick was not going to wake up.

Ricky and Ada Sue came into the room, found me sobbing, saw the chick in the window, and started to call me a murderer. They also called me silly because if Peep-Peep wasn't already dead; I was now freezing him to death. My mother took my hand, told my sibs to stop, and tried to soothe me. She said I was very smart because I thought about trying to get the chick some air. I began to feel better until my brother and sister began to reminisce about some ducks I supposedly had helped along on their journey to the other side. I fed them too much cornbread when I was two years old in Alabama.

From all of this, I found that despite the darkness and hopeless feeling that often accompanies a cold wind, I committed to learn from mistakes, to do much better, and to just hang in there. The breeze will warm eventually.

WIND CURRENTS
There Is Nothing To Be Afraid of
Except Fear Itself

CALCULATIONS IN THE DARK

Before I started kindergarten, we moved to 65th Street and Drexel Avenue in the Woodlawn neighborhood of Chicago's South Side. Our apartment occupied the first floor of a greystone building. There were four rooms in line from front to back: Mother and Daddy's room, the living room with the apartment entrance, our room, and the kitchen. Another family lived upstairs, and the Hardwicks lived in the apartment in the front part of the basement.

Basements are mysterious, scary, endlessly enticing, and fascinating to little kids. They're filled with old paint cans, failed or postponed hobby projects, furnaces, coal storage bins, oil tanks, hot water heaters, and countless boxes, castoffs, and cobwebs. Basements are inhabited by appliances that make noises and turn on and off by themselves.

The basement is always the epicenter of strange noises. *"It's the water pipes." "It's just the furnace." "The house is settling."* At least that's what your parents tell you is making the noise. Dark, dark corners and concrete spaces have a light dusting of cobwebs. Finished basements have sections that are all spiffy and nice, with paneling and tiled or carpeted floors. Some even have an apartment like the Hardwicks' in our building. Still, there is always a door that leads to a basement space that's dark or poorly lit. There are always doors to places where monsters or your siblings can hide. There are always cobwebs, and everybody knows cobwebs and dust are the signs of monster hangouts, places that can go dark in the blink of an eye.

I didn't like basements. I was afraid of the dark and basements scared me. That made our basement a very convenient place for my brother and sister to engage happily in their sibling duty to incite terror in the youngest. (Just a quick aside: the job of the youngest is to hang in there long enough for puberty and hormones to work their magic. You grow so quickly that you catch up to your siblings in strength, stature, and possibly cunning overnight. Then, you can settle the score. There are a few other ways for younger siblings to teach older siblings lessons of humility even before then. More on that later!)

I was intelligent, precocious, tall for my age, nosy, and always ready to participate despite the dangers. Even if I was frightened, I was still "game" if it meant I could hang with the older kids. Let me amend that. I was IQ-test smart, but maybe not too bright. I was always good for a laugh. Wait, wait, wait. I want to change that one more time. I was bright. But so were my brother and sister. And they were three and four years older than I was. That meant they would always be bigger, stronger, and faster than me and could find new ways of fooling me. They were not old enough to feel that getting a few good laughs at my expense, blood pressure, and heart rate was morally and ethically wrong.

Back to basements. Now, the basement on Drexel Avenue was particularly diabolical. It ran the entire width and a third of the length of the building. In that 15-by-30-foot space was a furnace with a coal storage bin against the right wall. An old oil tank with a water heater lurked on the left. Snuggled into the front left corner was an old wringer-type washing machine. Towels, sheets, blouses, pants, and underwear hung to dry on clotheslines that crisscrossed the open space in the center. The door to the Hardwicks' apartment was all the way front on the left wall. Hovering in the center of the rear wall was the solid wooden door leading to the crawl space underneath the house. It, in turn, was immediately adjacent to the outside storm door and the concrete stairs that led from the basement to the backyard. Altogether, it was a menacing tableau.

So why would sane children ever venture there? Parents! There were tasks, chores, and missions to be accomplished requiring our presence in the basement. Getting to the Hardwicks' without going out going out the front door and into bad weather meant one had to traverse this space. Mrs. Hardwick often looked after us, and we would play with her kids, Laurie, John L., and Paul. "Go get the dry clothes and bring them upstairs," was a parental command that also meant a trip to the basement. "Where's Tiger? Maybe the cat's in the basement," was another. To give me courage, my mother would always say things like, *"There's nothing to be afraid of except fear itself."* Or, *"There's nothing down there."* Or, *"You can carry your own personal protection and strength with you."* None of that really fortified me enough to go. Finally, Mother would say, *"Look, Mae, just go get the clothes,"* and that worked.

At times like these my analytical skills were tested. Should I chance the dangers of the dark and the deep alone, without my big brother and sister? Should I risk the possibility of disappearing unnoticed into oblivion and encountering the unknown bogeyman? Or, should I travel with untrustworthy partners, who could keep the monsters at bay, but who would willingly sacrifice me to them temporarily for a few laughs if I let my guard down?

I would choose the second, assuming I could use my strength, speed, and wits to anticipate when secret signals would flash between Ricky and Ada Sue. With luck, I could beat them to the top of the stairs and into our apartment before they could slam the door shut, lock it, and turn off the basement lights from inside the apartment leaving me alone on the stairs. I do not know the percentage of times that my strategy worked, but I do remember the times when I was trapped in the basement, in the dark ... alone.

Suffice it to say, a good, strong, healthy six-year-old heart that restarts automatically was important to my being here to tell this tale today. How the rest of my organs functioned without blood I do not know. During the hour that my heart stopped, I stood petrified on the stairs. My brain and the rest of my body continued to function. My mouth screamed. My eyes teared. I tried furiously to calculate whether it was possible to get to the bottom of the steps and turn on the light from the basement without the creature that lived in the coal bin reaching between the stairs and grabbing my leg. How could I evade the primordial forms under the oil tank that would slither out to grab me as I tippy-toed up to pull the light cord? My deliberations always led me to hope monsters didn't know how to climb stairs or that maybe they would stumble. Then Ada Sue or Ricky would open the door and almost fall on the floor laughing. My heart would start, along with the swup-swupping, and I would vow to be more on my guard next time.

I still don't like basements. But I learned they exist for good reasons. They are most common in the North because the foundation of a building needs to be below the depth where the ground will freeze in the winter. Basements are good for storage. Cats like to hide there. You can fix basements up and put exercise rooms in them. And besides being damp and dark, they're really not that scary. Get to know one during the light of day and look around. It's fun to understand all the pipes, vents, and electrical conduits that are housed in basements. Even the goblins are pretty cool.

I was a "scaredy-cat" as a little girl. And I am so amazed when folks call me brave these days. I always thought of myself as a chicken. I would try most things because I was curious. It wasn't that I had no fear, I just needed to know. My curiosity made me put trepidation aside and explore. Of course, I always had a quick exit scoped out.

KEEP LOOKING FORWARD AND SMILE!

I love movement and generally can hardly sit still. As a girl, I would turn flips, jump up and down continuously, and put on a "dance show" at the family gatherings. I always knew how to do the latest popular dances. The "Four Corners," "Bugaloo," "Mashed Potato," "Popcorn," and "Skate." When I saw professional dancers like Lola Falana, Joey Heatherton, or Cyd Charisse dancing on television, I was mesmerized. Ada Sue took piano lessons. My mother signed Ricky up for accordion lessons (yep, you know, Lawrence Welk, polka) and karate lessons. Then, it was my turn. I constantly begged to take dance classes. I would do anything to take them. *"Please, please, pleeeasse! I really want to do it."*

Besides being very kinetic as a child, I was also known among the relatives as being clumsy. I stumbled and fell frequently when walking down the street and climbing or descending stairs. My shins were always host to fine exhibition of wounds, scabs, and scars; fresh, middle-aged, and healed. My "run-ins" with gravity were a constant source of amusement to my siblings.

Once, when I was leaving the movie theatre, I was talking and trying to keep up with Ada Sue and Ricky at the same time. I stumbled, fell, rolled, and skidded 20 feet downhill from the refreshment counter to the entrance of the Maryland Theater. A legend was born. *"From the candy stand to the ticket man,"* was a refrain sung over and over by my siblings to celebrate that particular public tumble. In fact, they made up a whole song that still sends Ada Sue, now a child psychiatrist, into peals of laughter.

"Please, please, pleeeasse! I really want to do it."

My mother thought that ballet and dance classes would teach me to be graceful and diminish my tendency to trip over things.

"Please, please, pleeeasse! I really want to do it."

Finally, it worked. When I was eight years old, my mother and I went to the Sadie Bruce Dance Academy on 54th and Calumet Avenue. I signed up for beginning ballet. I got little black ballet shoes, leotards, and tights. "Excited" isn't adequate to explain how I felt. I was thrilled, enchanted, all smiles.

I would take class at 10:30 every Saturday morning. I was entrusted to take the "El" train by myself. It was called the "El" because it was elevated off the ground; it didn't run underground like the subways in cities like New York and London. I would walk about four blocks from 65th Street and Drexel to 63rd Street and Cottage Grove Avenue, to get to the "El" station platform. Then I would tiptoe up the stairs to the first level, keeping my eyes focused straight in front of me. I would not look down under any circumstances. I would pay my fare and climb the rest of the way up to the platform to the train tracks. I'd always stand as far from the street side of the platform as possible without getting too close to the edge where the train would come. I would avoid looking down because I didn't want to glimpse the street between the wooden slats of the platform. Just that glimpse would have destroyed my self-induced illusion that I was not 20 feet above the street. This future astronaut was afraid of heights! Then I would take the B train four stops to Garfield Boulevard and Wentworth Avenue. After I carefully made my way down from the platform to the street, I would breathe a sigh of relief, realizing I had controlled my fear long enough to accomplish something I wanted: to learn to dance. I would cross busy Garfield Boulevard, 55th Street, and walk over to the house that hosted the dance school in the basement.

The assistant teacher would first put my class through our paces in a small side room. Its silver painted walls always fascinated me because the swirl of the brush strokes formed a pattern that enveloped the room. That's where we learned the basics of ballet: feet positions, arms, posture, and some of the dance steps. Then the whole class would go to the big studio, where Sadie Bruce herself would instruct the class.

Miss Bruce was always intimidating to me. She was a short, stocky woman, who looked strong as nails and never seemed to smile. And in side room you could hear her screaming at the older kids. But she always had something provocative to say about dance, something to make you think. She talked about Red Skelton. Skelton, a famous slapstick comedian with a weekly television show, parodied ballet dancers. Miss Bruce made us understand that in order to mock dancers so effectively, Skelton himself had to have a keen understanding of ballet. Like I said, she made you think.

As a dancer, Miss Bruce was tough on us: *"Don't clump around like a horse." "Land lightly on your feet." "No one wants to see you grunting and groaning; they want to see smiles." "Your dance should be effortless."*

Later, I learned that we were practicing for a dance recital. We took letters home to our parents stating how much our costumes would cost, when we would be measured for them, how much deposit was required, and most importantly how to order tickets for the recital.

My very first ballet recital! We wore pink toile tutus with satin bodices that had silver bric-a-brac across the straps and top. Small pink net flowers danced on the bodice. We also had to have pink ballet shoes. To save money, my mother and I spent the morning of the recital painting my black ballet shoes pink and hoping we didn't miss any spots.

Posters for "The Sadie Bruce Dance Revue" appeared in public places all over the South Side of Chicago. The recital was held at the Chicago Opera House, and it was huge—both the opera house and the recital. I never knew that there were so many students at the dance academy!

The afternoon of the performance, Mother came backstage and put rouge and lipstick on me. She helped me get dressed. Then she left to go and sit in the audience. I don't really remember how the dance school instructors got us in place to go on stage, but I do remember seeing the bright lights, a huge stage, and what looked like endless darkness beyond. I knew Ada Sue, Ricky, Daddy, and Mother were out there, but I had no idea where. I concentrated on my steps. I didn't miss any and I remembered to look forward and smile.

The second year, following the recital, my mother decided to take me out of the Sadie Bruce Dance Academy, because she felt the emphasis was not on teaching the students how to be good dancers, but on putting as many bodies into costumes and onto stage as possible. My mother then enrolled me in modern dance classes with Michelle Madison at the Jane Addams Hull House Association Community Center on 67th Street and Eberhardt Avenue, where I was already taking ceramics and art classes.

Mrs. Madison was a beautiful young Black woman in her

early twenties, who looked like my vision of a dancer. She came to class with her leotards and tights under a long wrap skirt or a short miniskirt. She wore a stylish warm coat and boots. She was conscious of her body and her carriage in a very unself-conscious manner. Her arms, back, and torso were muscular but she was lithe, liquid, and smooth. She was strong, with delicate, graceful movements. She sweated. Her body exuded confidence. It was neither timid nor afraid.

Every Saturday morning, Mrs. Madison would work us very hard with basic dance movements, techniques, and exercises. There I learned precisely what a contraction, arch, flat back, point, flex, and plié should look like. We did pike sit-ups, held relevés, and worked on our "turn-outs." Then, we would learn complicated dance routines that always challenged me to understand shape, form, and rhythm. Mrs. Madison would correct my movements and make me hold them. I grew stronger with her. I gained an appreciation for hard work, physical strength, and grace that has stayed with me through the years.

Lola Falana, watch out!

SIROCCO
A Hot, Intense Wind

Stoop sitting was a major pastime for kids in Chicago in the summer. A stoop was any place outside of the house that was big enough for more than one body to occupy. A stoop could support a small congregation. A stoop needed to be close to the sidewalk. The perfect stoop was a small porch that led directly to the sidewalk or a doorway with a small step for a landing on apartment buildings. Congregations often centered on the concrete stairs leading up to the entrances to the greystone buildings. At times, it seemed everybody and his brother would be sitting out on the stoop when you needed to pass. The gang members particularly seemed to like stoops.

I really didn't have any qualms about walking past the stoop congregations when I was six, seven, eight, nine, or ten years old. But one day, coming back from my friend Jackie's house on University Avenue, the lead stoop sitter in a bunch of stoop sitters called out to me. I was wearing my favorite outfit: little red shorts, a red and white checkered midriff blouse, and tennis shoes with red sweat socks. The stoop sitter asked how old I was. I replied ten. Then he asked if I had an older sister and did she look like me. I was afraid to lie. So, I said "yes." He told me to make sure I brought her with me the next time. They all smiled, laughed, and gave high fives. From then on, I took a much more circuitous route to my friend Jackie's apartment. I became wary of walking in front of groups of guys on the stoop. My sister never went there with me. I told my mother. I don't think she told my father. He was someone who took action.

It was under much more serious circumstances that both my parents acted, changing our lives. The confrontation between my brother and members of the Blackstone Rangers gang compelled us to move out of Woodlawn immediately. The incident happened so quickly, early on a warm Chicago summer evening.

There were always stories of gang fights going around the neighborhood, and sadly, every so often, the tale of a boy who had been stabbed or shot with a zip gun. At Wadsworth Upper Grade Center, the middle school my brother and sister attended, there was a story of one boy having his testicles cut. The images of blood and pain filled my mind, even though I was still in grade school.

In our neighborhood, there were certain rules. If folks heard there was to be a gang fight, everyone would clear the street. At night, occasionally, one would hear a popping sound, possibly shots. Rule: turn off the lights and hit the floor until everything was over for a least 5 to 10 minutes. No, do not put your head up and try to peek out the window. The frequency of the stories and war drills gradually increased.

Drexel Avenue was very close to the border between the Blackstone Rangers and Disciples gangs' territories. The street gangs believed that everyone should be a member. They actively recruited any young man, especially if that youngster looked tough. If the teenage boy did not go along with their dumb behavior, someone was to teach the young man a violent lesson. Young men had to choose sides.

My brother, Ricky, had grown quickly. By the time he was 12 years old, his nickname was "Bear" because he was muscular, dark-skinned and handsome. At Wadsworth everyone thought he was older. He was chosen to attend an early involvement program at Hyde Park High School to learn to play the bass fiddle. He was accosted regularly by the Blackstone Rangers as he walked or rode the bus back and forth.

By the time he was 14, Ricky had grown to look considerably older. He went to Lindbloom Technical High School, a magnet school outside of our district. So, none of the gang members around our neighborhood knew him as a cohort. Besides, my mother and father would not have tolerated Ricky being in a gang in any form or fashion. Period. But my Daddy "didn't raise no punk," so this particular afternoon was bound to happen.

Our usual circle of friends—Ada Sue, Ricky, the Allen kids from next door, the Mitchells from across the alley and I— were sitting out on the front porches of our building and the Allens' house. Yeah, we were stoop sitting. Talking, jumping Double Dutch, playing tag, playing teenagers being cool. Ada Sue, Zandra, Sheldon, Artie, Roxanne, and Ricky were all in high school. Debbie, Stanley, Joe Joe, and I were preteens, just getting ready to start middle school. Debbie and I were on the sidewalk jumping rope or playing hopscotch. My brother, Artie, and Sheldon were sitting on the stoop of the Allens' house. Stanley was sitting on our porch. Just a lazy spring afternoon on Drexel Avenue, until about six older teenage boys eased down the street. One openly carried a chain. Another toted a pipe.

Everyone paused as these teenagers approached. They stopped in front of the Allens' house and said something to Ricky. He stood up. Words started to pass. I don't remember all the comments, but I do remember standing, and not saying anything. Maybe my feet were stuck. We waited to see what would happen, all eyes were riveted to the confrontation.

Danger doesn't register the same with all people. The conversation between my brother and these gang members, one with a chain, another with a lead pipe, became more heated. Everyone started to get nervous, afraid. How would I help? It couldn't really be serious, could it?

I jumped at the noise behind me. Our front door flew open and a woman's voice boomed, *"What the hell is going on out here?"* There was my mother, standing in the door with a pistol, very serious. Everyone's mouths dropped open.

One of the gang members immediately said, "Nothing, nothing." The leader attempted to find his bravado and said, "We were just talking."

Mrs. Dorothy Jemison, school teacher at Beethoven Elementary School in the Robert Taylor Homes projects by day, and mother of a 14-year-old black boy growing up in inner-city Chicago, at all times brooked no backtalk. She merely stated, get the hell away from my son and this house. *"Don't let me see* you *little hoodlums around here again. Don't ever talk to my son again, or you will have to deal with me and his daddy."* In an effort to salvage a bit of dignity, the teenagers tried to pimp off—that is, they strutted with a slight limp as if one leg was slightly shorter than the other. They walked slowly, but they left.

All of us began to talk excitedly. How did our mother find out? She had been in the kitchen cooking. My mother told Ada Sue, Ricky, and me to come inside the apartment right then. It was not for protection; it was for a conversation. Ada Sue and I had some very important questions to answer. My mother wanted to know why she had to be informed by Stanley that some gang members were confronting our brother?

It seems while everyone else was watching the show, Stanley who was one of those "fraidy-cat" kids, but who was actually quite smart, had had the wherewithal and sense to notice a dangerous situation and slip into our apartment. He shouted, "*Mrs. Jemison, there are some Blackstone Rangers out there trying to beat up Ricky."*

My mother wanted us to understand that her signal to action should have been from my sister or me. We should not have been gawking. This had been a very dangerous and volatile situation, and we should have informed her. We already knew that if one of us ever got into a fight we were expected—

no, required—to help out. It didn't matter how big the other kids were. But we were also expected to use good judgement and get someone who could help. Ada Sue and I were punished for lack of action in this situation.

My mother called my father at work and told him what had happened. Daddy came home straight away. Daddy, Mother, and Ricky got into the car and drove around the neighborhood looking for the gang members. My father wanted to reinforce my mother's message. Unbeknownst to me, once my father had followed my brother on the way to the Hyde Park High School program when he was in seventh grade. My parents wanted to understand why Ricky had been having attendance problems and poor grades. My father saw his 12-year-old son being harassed by two high school students on the way to better his education. Though my father believed in his son learning to fight his own battles, he also took care of his family. So Charlie Jemison, a.k.a. "Sideburns," got out of his car, collared these teenagers and let them know in no uncertain terms that they were never, ever to bother this particular boy. Ever.

After the confrontation on the stoop, my mother was absolutely adamant that we move from Woodlawn. The rapidity with which she made arrangements is only clear to me now. That September, before I had even attended Wadsworth Upper Grade Center for more than three weeks, we left 65th and Drexel where I had lived for seven years and moved into Morgan Park on 112th near Vincennes. We moved from the all-black ghetto (as that area, Woodlawn, was beginning to be called), to become the first back family on a block in this far South Side neighborhood. Though Morgan Park High School and a couple of the elementary schools had historically been integrated, the residential areas were not.

In our new home, I could hear the sound of freight train horns in the night. There were rabbits in the backyard and trees and lawns everywhere. The street in front of our house was brick cobblestone. I sat in Esmond Elementary School next to blonde white girls who looked like some of the characters out of *The Brady Bunch* on television. No one at Esmond had ever seen a girl like me with a short natural hairdo up close.

At Esmond, the principal appeared to have a hard time understanding the notes that accompanied my records from Wadsworth. My homeroom teacher there had recommended placing me in eighth grade rather than seventh, because my scores were all above senior level in high school. My former teacher had observed me and felt I had little to gain from the seventh grade. She had started the process of skipping me into eight grade before we moved. The Esmond principal couldn't comprehend that, with me coming from the inner city. So, he put me in the smart seventh grade class. When my new homeroom teacher, Mr. Zaber, saw the notes and my scores, he put me into his section of the eighth grade and in his class-room. He made sure I was challenged in math and science. The school had to put me into the smart eighth grade reading section.

As I rode the new bicycle I had received for my twelfth birthday through the unfamiliar streets of Morgan Park and surrounding areas, I felt a fresh gust of adventure.

SOLAR WINDS

HOW AND WHY ...

In first and second grades, I could not wait to do a science project. Ada Sue and Ricky had projects: an erupting volcano made with baking soda and vinegar, a working stop light. I hung around my father and mother helping them to help my 'sibs'. Sometimes I thought I was more interested in the projects than Ada Sue and Ricky were, but it only seemed that way because I wanted one of my own so badly.

From third grade to sixth grade I had a science project called the Eras of Time. It was really a compilation of information about the formation and evolution of the universe. I don't know why I found the subject of this project so compelling, but I just did. And I still do.

I focused primarily on the evolution of life on planet Earth. In each one of a series of clear plastic sweater boxes, I depicted a different geological era of time on the Earth. You could call them dioramas. I went from the Azoic—nothing was really in that box because that's when the "big bang" supposedly occurred—to the Archeozoic, Paleozoic, and Mesozoic, and I ended with the Cenozoic, the era we are in right now. Every year, outside of class, I would research and learn more about the evolution of life on earth and enhance my boxes. My Paleozoic Era was basically an aquarium with fish and plaster "fossils" I made for trilobites since I couldn't find any real ones. In the Mesozoic Era, the age of dinosaurs of which the Jurassic period is a part, I tried to include plants that looked like what I imagined were plants of that time. To demonstrate teeth on early mammals, I had an opossum skull (a real one with the brain rattling around inside) that I retrieved from one of my father's hunting trips. I used it because it was cool and the closest thing I could get to a fossil in Chicago.

I loved this Eras of Time project. To prepare for it, I read about how Earth may have been formed out of nothingness. In fifth and sixth grade, I discovered the experiments of Drs. Urey and Miller, scientists at the University of Chicago who, among other things, tried to understand how life formed on

Earth. They passed discharges of electricity through chambers containing chemicals thought to be the Earth's atmosphere in its early years, when it was just a billion years old. They were attempting o imitate early weather conditions. Simple amine compounds were formed. These amine compounds may have been the precursors of the amino acids that today form all our bodies' proteins. I read book after book on dinosaurs and evolution. I read how humans and other animals seem to have been in continuous evolution from one to another. I learned that as animals on this planet, we are much more related to one another than is immediately obvious. All these concepts were well within my ability to imagine and understand.

Well, maybe not. Understanding the beginning of the universe and nothingness is actually difficult. The size of infinity was tough to picture. I tried to imagine infinity, something that goes on forever, never ending. I tried to imagine nothingness—no energy, matter, light, dust particles—no anything—just nothing.

Attempting to grasp and expand on these ideas was fascinating. One thought lead to another. I couldn't stop thinking. What happens when I die? Is there really nothing? What is consciousness? What is the essence of me? Does it cease completely when I die? At times I thought I held the answer, but if I focused too hard it would all soon dissipate. Philosophy, the essence of life, religion, and questions about the purpose of existence, are kin to these concepts. Answers we chase even in the wind.

SEEING STARS

I went to a camp with my class for a week in March during the sixth grade. Chicago Public Schools sponsored the trip to get inner-city children more involved with nature. To help us prepare for the experience, my teacher, Mrs. Miller, made sure we learned the constellations and studied local birds. At camp I remember looking at the stars with her and drifting completely away. It was that sense of drifting away, yet belonging fully to the universe, that would take me to the library over and over to learn more about the stars.

Everyone in my family had library cards. Visits to the library were a constant part of growing up in Woodlawn and Morgan Park. From eight grade through high school I would often walk up the hill to the public library on Hoyne Avenue, about a mile away from my house. Sometimes I went with my sister, sometimes I went alone. Some of the books that I loved reading, I could not take out because they were reference books. I will just sit and read them in the library. They had wonderful color pictures. I was and remain absolutely fascinated by the stars, planets, and universe. I have always wanted to know more about cosmology, physics, theories on how the universe was formed, and the composition of stars. I learned about most of this by reading on my own. Sometimes the material was difficult to understand. For example, learning that scientists knew stars were made primarily of hydrogen because of the spectrum of light they emitted was a concept I understood after I researched the underlying topics. I would take out chemistry books, study them on my own, and get the information I needed to become more comfortable with the subject.

I often stayed at the library until it closed at 9 p.m. Walking home at night, I would look up at the stars. Though I was still afraid of the dark as a concept, walking outside at night and looking at the stars was liberating and not frightening. Cold nights were the best because the stars appeared even more luminous. This, I learned from astronomy books, was because the cold air had fewer heat refraction waves. As I walked, I imagined myself working at the Palomar Observatory in Southern California, which was the largest mirror telescope in the world at that time.

I have come to believe that my fascination with the stars is because of their timelessness. Stars have always been a part of the world, the universe. I read that the star which appeared in biblical stories at the time of Christ was probably a supernova, and that it may have also been recorded by Chinese astronomers. I read that people in the Southern Hemisphere see different stars than we do in the Northern Hemisphere, including the Southern Cross instead of the Big Dipper. While only logical, this difference spoke to the enormity of the universe and also to the many possibilities it holds.

I did not have a telescope as a child; I did not make one. I suppose I would've liked one, but they were too expensive. Fortunately, I did have Chicago's Adler Planetarium. There I got to see the stars of the Southern Hemisphere and what the night sky looked like one thousand, two thousand, and one million years ago during the time of dinosaurs.

Caught up in the vastness of the universe, I tried to imagine infinity as it had existed before and after the "Big Bang." Supporting the "Big Bang" theory was the observation of the "red shift" that told us the stars were moving away from us. The books said this "red shift" was akin to the Doppler effect for sound. The Doppler effect is what happens when a train moves towards you and the pitch of the whistle tone is higher; then, when the train travels away from you, the pitch of the whistle becomes lower. I read that Albert Einstein hypothesized that the universe was shaped like a saddle. Now how did infinity get to be shaped like a saddle? I wondered. I could not wait to take physics.

It was at the library that I picked up my first science fiction book written for grownups. I happened upon it while looking for astronomy books, which was what took me to the library most of the time.

Searching around for new books on astronomy, the beginning of the universe, galaxies, and stars with Greek mythological names brought me to Fred Hoyle. Hoyle, who was a British astronomer, wrote a novel called *A for Andromeda*. It was the name Andromeda, the galaxy closest to our own Milky Way galaxy, that caught my attention in the card catalogue. Back then, there was no internet and each library had file cabinets holding cards identifying each book as well as the its location according to the Dewcy decimal classification system.

In *A for Andromeda*, a radio telescope receives a signal that could not be a natural phenomenon. Its repetition and complexity had to be artificial. In the process of trying to decipher the signal, the astronomers discover that the signal is binary, that it is made up of ones and zeros, like a computer program. They build a computer, program it with this Andromeda galaxy software code, and watch what happens. The computer in turn builds a woman. As Sherlock Holmes says, "The game is afoot"—and I was hooked on science fiction. I read Hoyle's sequel *Andromeda Breakthrough* and then found other novels like *Colossus: The Forbin Project*. Books by Isaac Asimov and Arthur C. Clarke became staples. I started ordering from the Science Fiction Book of The Month Club.

Why was I hooked? Inside of each science fiction book I saw the hope that humans could do better, that we could advance. Mystery and adversity challenged our character. I found imagination, fantasy, and possibilities between the pages. Interestingly, as a young black woman, I identified with grown white men who were the main characters and heroes. I identified with the desire to understand the world. I wanted to place myself squarely in the fray and compete with my intellect, skills, courage, foolhardiness, and daring. The mystery was as important and inescapable to me as it was to them. That mystery was unifying.

I was not blind to the fact that often women were portrayed only as supporting characters. They were not scientists or adventurers, and when they were, they were not the heroes. Their actions were not pivotal to saving the day. To tell the truth, this pissed me off. Not enough to stop reading, but enough to know that only one side of the story was being told. Rarely, if ever was there an African, Indian, Chinese, Japanese, Hispanic, or any other person of color in the book. And if they did appear, they were never the scientists. Again, I knew better. There are sci-fi and adventure books that feature women and people of color by authors including Octavia Butler, Marion Zimmer Bradley, Anne McCaffrey, and Madeline L'Engle.

Madeline L'Engle was probably the first science-fiction author I read. In sixth grade I read the young adult novels *A Wrinkle in Time* and *The Arm of the Starfish*. They stand out as books that had women scientists and girl heroines. Those images were very important.

I loved the characters who were confident about their intelligence and were game for adventure. They loved and excelled in science as I did.

In medical school, I discovered Octavia Butler when I read an excerpt of the book *Wild Seed* in Essence Magazine. I was an instant fan. Butler, an African American woman, wrote novels flush with women heroines and people of color and explored concepts of how differing evolution of better sensing capabilities among people could be mistaken for mental illness. She imagined what would happen if a modern-day black woman got transported to the antebellum and the days of slavery.

Years later when I sat in the space shuttle waiting for launch, an incredible, huge grin came across my face. I smiled for that girl walking down Monterey Avenue on a cold, windy

Chicago winter evening, astronomy and adventure books tucked under her arm, neck bent back as she stared at the stars and a galaxy of signs.

CAUGHT IN THE EYE OF A HURRICANE

They say children ought not to have to go through some things. But I think it's how your parents, guardians, and the adults around you help you to process the incidents that makes the difference. The outcome of an experience depends on what you have inside of you beforehand. In certain ways, experiencing some hardships is easier as a child because you have more facility to heal. As long as the experience does not make you doubt your intrinsic self-worth, and you have someone, an adult, to help you remember the importance of love and caring, you may even be the better for it.

Under those circumstances, certain disturbances can build you into a more resilient, responsible person. You can begin to understand life from the point of view of the underdog, of those less fortunate, as well as that of the winner. You begin to differentiate the empty, harsh victory of the arrogant and privileged from the sweet, sustaining confidence of doing right. And you can begin to learn how to reconcile the difference between the philosophy of a system and its inherent worth, from those individuals who bend it to less noble ends. You can learn to commit yourself to doing better than that, even as the bile of indignation rises bitter in your throat; you can rally against your well-founded fear and anger. But you must have the right circumstances. I was lucky. I chose my parents, teachers, relatives, and birth year well.

I WAS ALWAYS BEAUTIFUL

My parents always discussed politics and social issues with us. After my mother saw Miriam Makeba, the South African singer, she felt compelled to celebrate our natural beauty. At that time in the United States, nappy hair, especially short nappy hair, was considered anathema to feminine beauty. Makeba brought to the United States, from apartheid-divided South Africa, the Xhosa tradition of women wearing their hair short to show the beautiful shape of their heads. For colored women, as "Black is Beautiful" took hold, Makeba's hairdo was a statement. A political, cultural, and self-esteem statement my mother declared we would make. At eight years old, I got my hair cut short and left nappy, in a natural hairdo. So did my sister. So did my mother.

Growing up I knew about Stokely Carmichael, H. Rap Brown, and *The Liberator* magazine. Malcom X and Elijah Muhammad were common names. We listened to Nina Simone, Olatunji, and The Last Poets; we read Ralph Ellison, James Baldwin, Lorraine Hansberry and Richard Wright. Around the kitchen table, discussion of Fidel Castro and the Bay of Pigs, the Soviet Union, and communism versus capitalism was *de rigueur*. We were forbidden to use the word "Black" as an insult as was often the case during that time; instead, "Black" became a word of pride. My uncle Louis philosophized on the words "colored" and "Negro." What was so wrong about being Black or African that we had to go to another language or euphemism to describe ourselves? Weren't white people of color too? My brother, sister, and I learned early on about Black history as a part of history, period. A Black man invented the traffic light. Paul Robeson was an athlete, scholar, and unparalleled opera singer. Madame CJ Walker became a millionaire selling products for black folks' hair. There were the Black Buffalo soldiers and Black cowboys and cavalry men.

My father was part Choctaw Indian. African slaves had

often escaped and had been aided by American Indians, often becoming part of their tribes. Black people accepted all the hybrids and mixtures of people into their community, too. Society considered as Black anyone who had Black ancestors, whether they were part white, mostly white, part Chinese, or Indian. But more important, the Black community accepted them. White people who were considered outcasts due to marriage to a colored person or for other reasons, were also taken in.

I was taught about tolerance. I was taught that just because someone else acts like a jackass, or is unfair, lies, or cheats, does not mean you should adopt his or her behavior. In fact, it seemed that the cornerstone of strength and continued faith for many Black people at the time was that they maintained the moral high ground in society. Uncle Louis and my mother particularly had frequent, long conversations about that. And about how as a Black person you better be twice as good as a white person to get anywhere.

The proverb "Two wrongs don't make a right" was well known in my home.

HELPLESSNESS, FRUSTRATION AND POWER

"*Black Power!*" When Stokely Carmichael chanted those words at a student rally in 1965, he meant economic improvement, confidence, self-esteem, and independence. The riots of the time didn't stem from that phrase, Black Power, but from built-up frustration. Neither my parents nor anyone else I knew participated in or believed that the riots that decimated some Black neighborhoods and businesses in cities across the nation during the summers in the 1960s were good. The riots did not directly help the Black community. In fact, they destroyed many of the Black businesses and single-family homes. Yet in a very real sense, the riots brought national attention to the serious problems of race and equality.

In spring 1968, after two previous summers of riots, television programs around the nation were interrupted with the news that Martin Luther King, Jr. had been shot and killed in Memphis. My parents predicted, "*It's going to be very hot this summer.*"

That summer the riots and destruction came closer to our home. In previous summers, it had mainly been the West Side of Chicago that had fallen into chaos. This time, stores only a couple blocks from our home were broken into and looted; shops on 63rd Street were burned. Curfews were imposed. Daytime was no longer safe. We all stayed indoors.

In 1968 the Democratic National Convention took place in Chicago with the attendant demonstrations. Mayor Richard Daley was determined to assert his control over the city.

Neighborhood streets were clear and empty even though it was the middle of the day. Complete stillness. The air was calm. There were no traffic sounds. A stray dog wandered across the vacant lot. Everything had that eerie feeling that comes with tornado warnings, but, instead of the pinkish-yellow hazy skies and humid air, the sky was blue, cloudless, and windless. It reminded me of the air-raid drills in school that prepared us for nuclear attack by the Soviet Union. We would walk quickly to the bottom floor, huddle inside corridors two students deep, and lean against the walls with our arms over our heads. I would wonder if the world would really end in a flash of light and a mushroom cloud.

This time I wasn't in school and this was no drill. I was at home peeking out the back screen door, deeply afraid to look outside, but too mesmerized not to. My 10-year-old heart was beating rapidly and my throat was dry, but I had to see. I had to run from the front picture window where I had a partial view of 65th Street, to the kitchen, where the vacant lot gave a clear view all the way over to Ingleside Avenue. I had to see.

And there they were: the National Guard, dispatched at

the request of Mayor Daley. Walking, and marching purposefully in a line while carrying rifles. They were dressed in fatigues, war costumes. They wore camouflage, combat boots, and helmets and held guns in front of them at the ready. Their orders were "shoot to kill."

My father was at work. I worried whether he would be safe on his way back home. The National Guardsmen did not seem to be there to protect *us*.

I was so scared peeping out. I was afraid the National Guard would see me. There were Black National Guardsmen too; I was also afraid of them. Children as young as 13 had been shot and killed during the riots. I knew as a 10-year-old Black girl that I was not precious to these adults. I believed they would kill me as readily as they would kill the Viet Cong the United States was at war with. It didn't matter that I was a United States citizen. It didn't matter that I was very smart, would probably grow up to be pretty like my mother, or that I was fun to talk to and had unlimited potential. It didn't matter that I was a good girl and hadn't been suspended from school. It didn't matter because *I* didn't matter to them. These adults, these representatives, and enforcers of the U.S. government, would hold me in suspicion and probably shoot me if I were out on the street. So I cowered behind the back door screen to see who they were. They looked like regular folks—but ready for war.

I was baffled and I was angry. I made myself a promise that I wouldn't be frightened like that anymore. I reminded myself I was as much a part of this United States as the Guardsmen or anyone else. I should expect as much from this country as they did. Goodness knows I was willing and determined to contribute; it was my right and responsibility. I just couldn't let folks blow up this planet. We, as humans, don't have that right. And we don't have the right to take other folks' lives and belongings or to frighten them, as I was frightened then.

As I said, the good thing about being a child is resilience. Soon things settled down, and we started going outside again. I forgot the fear and played in the vacant lot, ran errands for my parents up and down 65th and 63rd Street, and went to summer school. But I never forgot that feeling or the unspoken vow that I made in the summer of '68. It is vital to keep my humanity and my right to participate, but not to tread on the humanity and rights of others.

That unspoken vow has been so important in my life. As a civil servant, both as a Peace Corps physician and as an astronaut, I had to take an oath to the United States. I could do this not only because I recognized the opportunities, but also because I acknowledged my responsibility to help our country fulfill its promise. Even though, at the beginning of this nation, I would not have been recognized as a full person—

slaves were counted only as two-thirds of a person and, along with women, had no right to vote—I realized that the failure, the wrong was committed by the individuals, and not by the underlying philosophy of democracy. I have the right and responsibility to expand that philosophy and work to make it manifest. We all do.

WIND CURRENTS
An Extra Spoonful for Good Measure

In fourth, fifth, and sixth grades I started cataloging a number of ways that the world recognizes you as an individual, a full person, a human being with an identity. One is when folks ask your opinion and what you want. A stronger indication is when the opinion or what you want actually influences a decision. (Another seemed to be having enough money to buy more than just your lunch at school.)

One definite sign that you're an individual is when you get mail addressed to you, especially if it's from someone besides your grandmother. (Not that grandmother mail, great aunt, and older cousin mail isn't wonderful, but sometimes they write, you know, just to be nice or because they have to.)

Between the ages of 10 and 11, I figured out how to get other mail. It was really very simple. I couldn't believe no one else had thought of it. You merely had to fill in and mail the free offers in magazines for Book of the Month or Record of the Month clubs, the ones that said: "Nothing to buy. We will send you 12 books for 10 cents." Cool! However, I didn't read the part where you had to commit to buy other things to get such a great deal. Anyway, once you start, the books and mail addressed to you never stop coming. I was the envy of my older brother and sister until Ricky noticed that half the mail was addressed to "Mr. *Mac* Jemison" because someone did not write her name clearly. He got a good laugh out of that.

I got albums like *Mission Impossible* by Lalo Schriffin and *Hang 'Em High* by Hugo Montenegro. I joined the Science Fiction Book Club and the Science Book Club. I loved getting the mail, but I didn't understand why I kept getting threatening letters for payment until later. That was in the fine print that a precocious 10-year-old ignores. The incredible thing was that I got mail from companies I didn't even write to! That's how I received my first set of international recipe books. I don't even remember ordering them.

It was from these wonderful cookbooks that I tried many exciting recipes. I was already fairly good at cooking a few dishes with my mother, but none of those were deserts and sweets because we ate very few sugary things growing up. Therefore, when I needed a recipe for a special cookie that were sure to be a hit at the school bake sales, I consulted my cookbooks.

Small problem. Sometimes, many times, in fact, most of the time, I did not do a good job following the recipes. If I did not have a specific ingredient called for, I would substitute another I judged similar enough to work. And I couldn't always be bothered getting real measuring spoons and cups. I would "eyeball" measurements. The result? Cookies that would never brown. Cookies that turned very hard. Cookies that sold only one or two out of four dozen. Cookies that taught humility. Cookies that said, "Sometimes you have to learn to follow the rules."

UPDRAFT

Fall 1969. Miniskirts, platform shoes, and Afro hairdos were starting to be accepted. Martin Luther King Jr. and Bobby Kennedy had been killed the year before. Sit-ins and walkouts were common in colleges and schools across the country. "Soulful Strut" by The Young Holt Trio and "Love Land" by Charles Wright and the Watts 103rd Street Rhythm Band were my favorite songs, and The Temptations "I Can't Get Next To You" was not far behind. Improbable dances called the "Funky Chicken" and "Sophisticated Sissy" where the rage.

No other way to put it: my years in high school were tumultuous. I entered as a 12-year-old unknown freshman and quickly got on the wrong side of the vice principal. I graduated as a 16-year-old senior and student council president now firmly on the wrong side of that same vice-principal and perhaps a few other administrators as well. But there were teachers who were very proud of me and I had gained friends and respect.

Since sixth grade I had been at least 5'6" and somewhat thin. I had worn a short natural Afro since fourth grade. Sometimes folks mistook me for a boy because girls didn't have haircuts like that back then. It got a little rough during puberty when despite my budding mammary glands, well-meaning people in stores would call me "son."

You might think starting high school at age 12 sounds intimidating. Was it? Well, yes and no. It was scary because these were high school students, like my brother and sister. I went to a different class each period. There were lockers. Eventually I would be able to try out for cheerleading and plays. I would take physics, chemistry, and biology. Many more possibilities and options were available. It was cool that my brother and sister were at the same school. Ricky was particularly hip, and Ada Sue was president of the student council. I would get to do more strenuous sports and activities. I was already tall, so I didn't have to worry about being bullied because I was smaller than the other students.

Chicago has beautiful weather in September and early October. Crisp, clear days with autumn swirling in the air. I started school on such a day. My homeroom teacher, Mrs. Roberts, was very pleasant. She directed us to classrooms, and the cafeteria, and gave us our schedules. Mrs. Roberts was probably in her early forties, well-groomed and fashionably, but conservatively dressed. She wore her brunette hair in a flip. She took a liking to me.

My first few months at Morgan Park High School were a bit less than auspicious. It took a while to coordinate my energy, non-conformist streak, intellect, quick wit, and curiosity with the existing school structure.

Case in point: soon after school began, an assembly for about 400 members of the freshmen class was held to discuss school policy. I was sitting in a section with about 50 rowdy students, and we were told to remain in the seats when the assembly ended. We must have gotten a lecture on behavior, but all I remember is that about six of us couldn't produce our student IDs and had to report to the vice principal's office the next morning with the card in hand. Of course, I was one of those.

The next morning, I was the last to be called in by Mr. O'Bannon, the vice principal of student affairs. First, he asked me why I didn't have my ID on my person at the assembly. I answered, "Because, the ID was in my locker for gym, and 'my person' didn't have time to go get it before the assembly." Then he looked at my ID and asked "You're Ada Jemison's sister? I can't believe that." Mr. O'Bannon was the student council advisor and he was so proud of Ada because she was so smart and all the teachers adored her. Of course, I just smirked and blinked.

I had algebra, English, Russian, geography, art, study hall, lunch, and physical education. Believe it or not, my freshman year I got the worst grades and had the most difficult time in physical education. In fact, the first semester I got a D! How in the world do you get a D in girls' Phys Ed in Chicago in 1969, especially, when you are very athletic, like to dance, and are good in science and math? I could do sit-ups, count, and identify the parts of the body; if not for the health class portion, I probably would've gotten an F? How? Well, remember those cookies? You have to try hard to not follow instructions.

Here's how I did it. First, I didn't get my light blue, one-piece jumpsuit. When I finally got it, I did not sew my name on it quickly enough. I had a hard time polishing my gym shoes every week, keeping them nice and white with my name printed on the side. I was not really a slob, but I was just not as meticulous as Mrs. Branecki, my teacher, desired. Then there was swimming.

My mother didn't want me to take swimming, because of my allergies, but I really wanted to. I needed to submit a physician's excuse to exclude me for the year. I procrastinated and got a bad mark because I didn't have parental permission to swim or a doctor's note not to. It all ended happily though. By January, I had persuaded my mother to change her mind. I started taking swimming and progressed rapidly to the deep end. By my junior year, one-and-a-half years later, and after I had learned to keep my gym clothes presentable, I was chosen as a swim leader and a gym leader! And usually you didn't get to be a gym leader until senior year.

MY MO: GO FOR IT

One thing I was consistent about was testing limits—mine and those of other people, especially adults. I don't know if I was actually aware of what I was doing, but that's what I did. My modus operandi, my "MO," was to smile frequently and laugh whenever possible—including at myself. Life was fun. I imagined something I would like to do, particularly if I hadn't done it before. I would look around for a possibility and find a potential way to take advantage. Then I would figure out my best shot at accomplishing it. Then I'd go for it. Yeah! The All Chicago City High School production of *West Side Story* was the perfect opportunity.

I CAN'T SING, BUT I SURE CAN DANCE

I loved the musical *West Side Story*. It had a great plot, lots of great singing, incredibly cool dancing, and solid acting. Singing, dancing, and acting. I knew that I was very good at the second, could probably do the third, but that first one, singing, was a problem. I never could sing. As a child, I had been famous for my off-key renditions of "Jingle Bells." I could threaten people with "Rudolph the Red-Nosed Reindeer." However, I had heard Ethel Merman and a couple other Broadway stars sort of "sing-talk" their way through songs. At least, that was what it sounded to me. I had great stage presence, a good strong voice, and wonderful projection. I could make the folks in the back of the auditorium hear me! And I could dance! My favorite character in *West Side Story* was Anita, played in the movie by Rita Moreno. So, I decided to try out for the role of Anita. I pushed the limit with my "tongue planted firmly in cheek."

I found out what I would have to do to audition for the role of Anita. I would have to learn the scene preceding the song "America" with the character Bernardo (George Chakiris in the movie). Then I would have to sing "America" all the way through and be prepared to dance with the choreographer. "*Piece of cake*," I thought, "*I can do this.*"

I pulled out my *West Side Story* album from my Record of the Month Club contraband and listened over and over again to "America." I practiced Anita. I learned to sing-talk the words with a great Puerto Rican accent (at least *I* thought it was a great accent). My dialogue was fabulous, again with Puerto Rican accent, and I could already dance. The evening before auditions, I had my mother cornrow my hair. She still couldn't believe I had the nerve to try out for Anita—as I said, my singing voice was infamous. However, I was ready.

Saturday morning, I strode into the auditorium hall exuding incredible confidence. The girls were paired with various boys trying out for Bernardo. They weeded people out quickly. I read lines again, several times with the best male lead. Then they had us dance. "*Piece of cake*," as I said, I was a really good dancer. Finally, came the singing.

The director and music director sat together in the center of the auditorium. We were called on stage one at a time. After each person finished singing, each was told to sit in a certain section of the auditorium. As the auditions proceeded, it was pretty clear that the sections were equated with performance skill. My turn.

I exuded confidence. I had practiced this. I sauntered onto the stage. Anita was "attitude," if nothing else. I had my movements ready to go with the words. I sang. I sashayed. I smiled and strutted when finished. And I was told to leave the stage and go and sit behind the director. I didn't move. I asked to confirm, "Behind the director?" I couldn't believe it.

When I returned home my mother asked me how things went in her soft "motherly concern" voice. I told her I got called back for next Saturday and that they had placed me in a section with just several other girls. The girls who could really sing. My mother just shook her head. Ha! I had made it. Vindicated!

I worked even harder over the following week to be ready for the call back. About 10 girls were called back, including me. Since the show ran longer than a week, the directors were going to choose two girls to play Anita. All things being equal, I had a one in five chance; much better odds than before.

Saturday morning. Hair freshly cornrowed, a little bit of makeup, cheerful, bright-colored clothes, leotards and hip-hugging bellbottom pants, and plenty of smiles and attitude.

This time auditions did not take place in an auditorium, but rather in the dance studio of the high school downtown.

We danced. I did very well. We dialogued. Cool! Still looking good. Then they sent some of us over to the piano with the music director. We had to learn a new song. Now, I know exactly what you're thinking: "Busted!" But, I was still cool and confident because I was prepared. I had learned *all* of Anita's songs. I was ready to sing-talk my way to the winning part. I had contingency plans. I was not a Girl Scout, but I had come prepared.

The music director pulled out the music and played "Maria" or … I don't even remember, but it wasn't any song that Anita had ever remotely sung, not even in chorus. The jig was up. I just smiled, tried to learn it the best I could. When it was my turn to sing for the director, I gave it all I had, but the strained look that came over his face gave me a clue. He seemed to be trying to understand who this girl was and what had happened to the one who sang for him last week?

After the two Anita's were chosen, some of the other girls cried. I tried to comfort one whom I had become friends with the prior week. I just smiled, and laughed. I felt a bit like I had been caught with my hand in the cookie jar. I went home, and my mother saw me smiling and happy. She frowned and asked incredulously "Mae, you got the part?" All I had to say was, "They changed the song."

But I did end up with a part in *West Side Story*. Next I tried out for "Anybody's" (that was the character's name). She didn't sing. She was the tomboy who hung around the Jets. One small problem: at 5'8," 140 pounds, I was bigger than the guy they chose to play Riff, the Jets' gang leader. So, I ended up being a member of the Jets' gang's girlfriends. And I helped to design the costumes.

A SMALL PUSH AND A LOT OF NERVE

"No, I don't know what sickle cell anemia is."

"Then you need to look it up. You're always talking about space exploration. Why don't you think about something else?"

I hated it when she did that. Whenever my mother wanted me to try something, she didn't spend a lot of time telling me what it was or what to do, she just dropped the provocation on the table like a loaf of bread and left. I could pick it up and eat it if I wanted or I could starve. My choice. Not a lot of preamble, no warning, at least not any that I paid attention to. No real direction, and the older I got, the less direction I received and the more challenge and doubt of my abilities, seemed implicit in that casually dropped phrase or topic.

So there it was. Sickle cell anemia. Dropped on the metaphorical table. A challenge. She wasn't going to tell me. Since

I thought I was so cool and science-smart, a junior in high school, I should know. *Phooey*. She did this just because I said I wanted to do a science project. Just because I didn't want to work anymore with the goldfish swimming in mazes after being exposed to varying concentrations of thyroxin. So, what if the cats constantly went fishing in the bowls of fish that were scattered throughout the breakfast room? I always cleaned up the goldfish flipping and lying gasping on the floor. I knew it cost a lot to buy the goldfish. Okay, the project was a bit of a bummer—the little fish brains had a problem with mazes. But the project did lead me to do a lot of research on pyridoxine and the effects of thyroid hormone on learning, and I learned how to construct a maze with epoxy and acrylic pieces.

Oh well, this year: sickle cell anemia. When I again peeked, it was still just lying on that psychological table. No clues left behind. Why did she do that? I didn't know. Maybe to make my work harder than the challenges school provided. Darn I couldn't even gloat and say I knew what sickle cell anemia was.

So do some *research*. The dictionary said, "Sickle cell anemia is an inherited blood disease found primarily in people of African ancestry." Okey dokey. What do I do now?

I was 15, and I was confident that the world and people wanted to help. Or, at least, that I could talk them into helping me. Whom could I turn to for help with this? I knew that hematology was the study of blood diseases. I had once been to Cook County Hospital to visit my aunt, so why not call their lab?

"Just do it, Mae."

"Alright, alright."

"I don't have the number"

"So call the operator." I often had these two-sided dialogues with myself.

"There, the phone is ringing. *Are you happy?* It's not even the hematology lab. It's the main hospital telephone."

"Ask for the hematology lab."

"And what do I say when hematology answers? I don't ... Oh, Hello. My name is Mae Jemison. I am a junior at Morgan Park High School, and I'm working on a science project ... Oh, okay. Yes, I would like to speak to the chief hematology lab technician."

"Slow your breathing down. Do not hyperventilate. Just say ..."

"Yes, my name is Mae Jemison and I am working on a science project on sickle cell anemia ... Uh, huh. High school chemistry and biology. Yes, I read a lot, and I'm good at lab work."

"Yes, I have done science projects before. I would like to help."

"Yes, I can come .... Next Tuesday at 4:30 p.m. Sure."

"Mother, how do you get to Cook County Hospital?"

I was a little nervous. I had never taken the train and bus alone all the way from the South Side of Chicago to the West Side where Cook County Hospital Hektoen Hematology Labs were located over on Rush Street. In fact, to my recollection, I had never traveled to the West Side by train with or without anyone; we always drove over. By the time I took the 112th Street bus from in front of Morgan Park High School to the Dan Ryan train station at 95th and State Streets, then transferred to the "El" train and arrived at Rush Street, it was almost 4:30 p.m.

I met the technician at the 8th floor lab, slightly breathless, but profoundly impressed with myself for getting there on time. The technician, a middle-aged African American man, asked me what I knew about sickle cell and chemistry. At that point, I knew sickle cell disease was inherited through a recessive gene and could be fatal by the time a person became a teenager and that historically, very few people survived beyond their twenties with the disease. I also knew that people who had it suffered from frequent illness and infections, abnormal growth, and episodes of severe pain called "crises" in their joints and internal organs. I knew that the disease got

its name because, at times, the red blood cells of people who suffered with it were sometimes shaped like sickles or quarter moons instead of circles like normal red blood cells. But I didn't not know how it was diagnosed or treated. As I sat there this wonderful man told me how they diagnosed sickle cell anemia in the laboratories. He showed me equipment and quizzed me on pH and solutions: molar, normal, and volumetric. I did know some chemistry. I could tell he was impressed. He told me I should come in twice a week.

Over the next month, the technician taught me how to recognize the difference between the electrophoretic movement (how molecules move under the influence of electricity) of normal or A hemoglobin, sickle cell or S hemoglobin, and fetal or F hemoglobin. I learned what the movement pattern looked like that indicated a person had sickle cell anemia, sickle cell trait, normal hemoglobin, thalassemia, or sickle cell and thalassemia combined. (Hey, I know the words are big. But I had to look them up, so you should give it a try, too.) I made solutions for the entire laboratory and set up the electrophoresis chambers. I also learned how to do the preliminary test to see if it was even necessary to test the blood sample for hemoglobinopathies. (That's abnormal hemoglobin for those of you not in the know. Now that I was learning how to use these big words, I was *très* cool.) The lab tech was very impressed with how quickly I learned. So was I—within a month I had the jargon *and* the swagger.

Then one day, while standing next to the centrifuge, waiting for it to spin down so I could remove a sample, I looked up and there was this white, fortyish, male doctor looking at me. In fact, he was standing over me waiting for me to turn around.

I casually took my samples out of the centrifuge and said "Hello." He introduced himself as the head of the hematology department. He had a German or Swedish-sounding accent. (I couldn't distinguish any further, though by then I could recognize French, Spanish, British, Southern, East Indian, and nasal Midwestern twang.) He politely inquired who I was and what I was doing in the lab.

Not being overly timid, I answered with my name and politely stated that I was working on a science project on sickle cell anemia. I don't recall if he smiled or not, but the next words are imprinted on my memory. He asked quite simply, "What is your hypothesis?"

For the second time in this particular science project adventure, someone, not even my mother this time, had me at a loss for words. After moving my mouth and trying to find an answer, I said I was doing a demonstration project. I knew how to do all this lab work. The doctor replied: "No. If you are going to work in my lab on a science project, you will have to develop a hypothesis, do more background research, and experimentation." He relieved me of my samples, gave them to one of the lab techs, and took me to his office. We discussed a bit more of my background and what a science experiment entailed. Of course, I knew about hypotheses, scientific method and experimental protocols. I just didn't have one. He gave me assignments to look up a couple of authors and scientific papers and to contact the National Institutes of Health. I had to research more information on the biochemistry of sickle cell anemia in order to determine a compound that might reverse sickling.

I look back now and wonder if I had been set up all along. The head of the hematology department had another student working in the lab on blood typing. He also did not appear to be a person who did not know what was happening in his lab. Over the next few months, I spent many hours, and Saturdays and Sundays at the Illinois Institute of Technology library. I wrote to the National Institutes of Health and they wrote back and sent me scientific paper reprints! I struggled through original scientific articles that discussed theories about why red blood cells sickled, why the sickle cell trait could sometimes be dangerous, and the effects of low concentrations of oxygen and temperatures on hemoglobin S. These were the circumstances under which the red blood cells changed shape. And I learned that Dr. Linus Pauling, called the father of modern day biochemistry, had earned the Noble Prize for his work showing that sickle cell anemia disease was caused by the substitution of a single valine amino acid molecule in the sixth position of the normal hemoglobin amino acid sequence. That single substitution caused all the problems. Through this discovery, Dr. Pauling was able to demonstrate that it is the linear sequence of amino acids that determines the 3-D shape of a protein and its physiologic function. Cool. I didn't know people actually studied Black folks' disease. And here was a study that was fundamental to understanding biochemistry.

Through discussion with the physician, I decided on a compound to test that might inhibit sickling. And we tested it! All of this information I had to find and digest. Many times, I had to learn other stuff just to really understand one sentence in a medical journal article. I was jazzed!

Closing in on the date of the science fair, the head of hematology demanded to see my exhibit. He also required me to write and type (no computers or word processors available in those days) a scientific paper. It was most embarrassing when once he, a non-native speaker of English, corrected my spelling—I bet him and lost. I learned about art transfer letters, how to get photographs from microscopes, and statistics.

Whew! He was tough and did not accept "pretty good." He expected excellence. Period. Nothing less. I was surprised that this European doctor showed so much interest in my work, and allowed me to work in his lab. He seemed to really want me to work in his lab. While I was occasionally intimidated by his knowledge and the graduate-school-level tasks, I always spoke up and would try even harder to be prepared the next time. At fourteen and fifteen, I was comfortable being accepted as his colleague.

Perhaps, the most lasting impression of this experience is that by taking a chance on being hung up on and refused and working with the unfamiliar, put me in touch with people willing to take that same chance on me. Sucking up my feelings of "Wow, can I do this?" and just trying, risking, and being willing to put in the effort to accomplish the tasks led the way to one of the most positive, enabling experiences in my entire life.

Oh, yeah. I almost forgot about what started all of this. What happened at the science fair? I got an "Excellent" at the City-Wide Chicago Public School Science Fair held at the Museum of Science and Industry. As a result, I was invited to exhibit as the public school representative at the Field Museum of Natural History, during a city-wide private school science fair, and I won first place.

STUDENT COUNCIL: "Y'ALL ARE WITH ME, RIGHT?"

I really pushed the limits my senior year as president of the Morgan Park student council with the homecoming parade. I didn't realize until years later, that it was because of the road-blocks placed by an adult "adversary" which we had to clear that led us to success.

I could not believe our faculty advisor was scolding us. After all the hard work and fun everyone had had. The way the pieces of the puzzle had all come together. We had the right to celebrate. To me, it seemed our faculty advisor was just upset because we pulled it off without him, while he had stood back and thought that we—translate me—would fall on our faces.

My answer was, "Mr. O'Bannon, do not stand here and say these things to *my* student council. If you have any problems, you talk to me." I said this in front of everyone. Isn't that what a leader is supposed to do? Stand up for the troops and take the flack?

The other students swiveled their heads back and forth, as they looked at me standing up to Mr. O' Bannon, the vice principal in charge of student council. Yeah, that Mr. O'Bannon, with whom I had had problems since our first run in when I was a freshman. A Black man in his 40s, he even recruited a white male student to run against me for student council president. (Interestingly, the boy O'Bannon chose was one of my friends, who told me his heart wasn't in it.) I do not know why I did not get along with him. Mr. O'Bannon liked my sister, who had been student council president three years before. He was even friends with my brother now. But me, no way.

Yet, I still could write hall passes for students. I guess Mr. O'Bannon knew that I would never help anyone cut class. That rigid, principled backbone inside of me went both ways, and as a teenager I applied it ruthlessly.

Which brought us to the homecoming situation. I was indignant that he did not say, "Job well done," but rather seemed to berate us because we did it without him. In fact, the whole thing was pulled off in an impossibly short amount of time, with occasions of—how shall we say—not particular grace.

Sometime in the early fall, during our student council class period, the idea of the homecoming parade came up. It sounded wonderful. But it gained even more appeal when Mr. O'Bannon said, "No way." So, of course we insisted. Then he said he would have nothing to do with it. Even better. I loved a good antagonism, back then at age 15. When I was a teenager, it was easier to put people in strict categories of good or bad. Looking back, I now realize it was extraordinary that Mr.

O'Bannon allowed us to attempt holding a parade, when it was against his better judgment. He must have had a certain faith in us and was willing to let us learn the lesson that he felt was awaiting us. I appreciate the patience required to deal effectively with individuals as they search for the limits of their capabilities and others' tolerance. I was fortunate to have had safe outlets for my rebellious inclinations.

Football season. I loved football. I even had a uniform for a football games: blue jeans, a kelly green shirt with tons of school pins, a kelly green derby, grey Hush Puppy type shoes, and a white nylon jacket. Morgan Park's colors were green and white. The team's mascot was the Mustang, and I had green-and-white pom-poms leftover from my freshman and sophomore years as a pom-pom girl.

Homecoming parade. *Sounds great! What do we have to do?* Floats, marching band, and decorations. We had to ask the shop and art classes to help out. We needed to raise money. We tried to make money selling buttons with the school's mascot on it, but the button manufacturers printed a draft sketch. Disastrous, but we tried to sell them at a discount to the feeder elementary schools. What else? To Mr. O'Bannon's credit, he would raise stumbling blocks about problems that required solutions when we didn't even know the problems existed. An example: Who knew you needed a parade permit?

So one October day, Lynda Bundrage, my best friend and the vice president of the student council; Jimmy Sparks, a friend with a car; and I found ourselves downtown on our way to City Hall. It was a football game day for Morgan Park. Jimmy Sparks was about 6'2," maybe weighed 150 pounds soaking wet, and he was the drum major of the school band. He was dressed in his drum major uniform, I, of course, had on my green and white football outfit and Lynda was dressed for football, too.

Chicago is known as the Windy City and the wind was howling down Michigan Avenue that day. As we walked down the street, the tails of Jimmy's white drum major jacket flapped in the wind. Lynda struggled to keep up as Jimmy and I walked quickly towards City Hall to apply for the parade permit. When we arrived, all windblown, the clerk there asked us if we were dressed for Halloween. When you're with two other people, hey, what is humiliation?

FINDING A PLACE

For me, the most peculiar aspect of being a teenager and going to an integrated high school in Chicago in the early seventies did not center around "finding myself." I knew who I was. I knew about as well as anyone with swirling hormones, increasing shoe size, shifting family status, and added responsibilities could. Rather, the peculiar part was not allowing others—adults and students, blacks and whites—to stick me inside a particular box just to make it easier for them to categorize me. If they could, then they would not have to see, talk to, respond, and deal with me, the individual.

I tended to complicate the box problem a bit more for people. I was a feminist and excelled in and aspired to careers in both science and dance. I was outspoken. I was basically happy, forgiving, moderately well read, not a "druggie," radical and a little square and willing to take stands and risks.

For example, my junior year, I went from being the darling of advanced placement U.S. history class, when we studied the policies of *laissez-faire,* to the teacher's to major provocateur and class hell-raiser when we approached slavery and the modern era. In fact, my friends said that they came to class to see what would happen during the "Mae and Mr. Meade Show" each morning.

My friends reflected my range of interests and the many places I felt comfortable. Here is the rundown of my high school friends, my crew, posse, "homeys," gang, buddies, whatever. Not listed in any particular order.

Kathy Sharpe and I were an unlikely pair. Kathy was a blue-eyed platinum blonde, and stocky, about 5'1."

Kathy and I took Russian together for four years, and were pom-pom girls our freshman and sophomore years. Kathy could usually get her family car and we'd drive around in the evenings always ending up at White Castle on 127th Street and Western Avenue in Blue Island to buy hamburgers and onion rings. Kathy and I talked about all kinds of things from boys (ones we liked and those who didn't give us a second look) to teachers, and more philosophical concerns like science fiction and what the world would be like in the future.

I learned to play ping-pong at Kathy's house. Her little brother was fun sometimes, but mostly omnipresent and irritating. (Was that what I was like to my brother and sister?) Once while walking with Kathy down my block on the way to her house, we passed an older black teenage boy sitting on his porch. He asked me why I didn't hang with my own kind. My block had changed from all-white to primarily black in the three years since my family first integrated it. Funny, I thought Kathy was my kind. She was a smart, athletic, courageous, and out-of-the-box thinker like me. Without being naïve, I thought certainly Kathy was at least as close to "my kind" as he was.

I met Kathy at Esmond Elementary School, when I first moved to Morgan Park, but we became close friends in high school. I heard from her frequently when we first went off to college. She majored in forestry in college and, for a while, was a forest ranger. She was absolutely "my kind."

Once the high school dress code that required girls to wear skirts and dresses was eliminated, Sheila Wang and I were the two girls in school who were never seen in anything but pants. Sheila's father was from China and her mother was a white

American. Sheila and I were the political rebels in our class and were both quite good in math and science. In fact, my senior year, each morning at 7 a.m. before regular classes started, Mr. Drymiller met with us to teach us solid analytic geometry and calculus. At the end of our junior year in Algebra III and Trigonometry, Mr. Drymiller offered to teach us, on his own time, the advanced mathematics we would need to know to be successful as we entered the universities we would probably attend. We jumped at the chance. At the time I did not realize what a special effort Mr. Miller was making. But later, I understood just how important his effort was to my academic and professional development. And, truly, how incredible it was for a teacher to give so much of his time. Sheila and I hung out a lot junior and senior year as well. Sheila earned her Ph.D. in physiological psychology and had three children. We renewed our close friendship years later.

Denise Thomas, also known as Dee Dee, became a New York trial lawyer and co-developer of the off-Broadway musical *A Brief History of White Music in America*. The musical featured popular white music hits over the years from "How Much is that Doggie in the Window" to "I Wanna Hold Your Hand" but sung by black singers with a soulful vibe. It's great music with a fresh, and enlightening turn-about is fair play twist to an old theme. It parodied in an entertaining way how white singers made hits of black music—think Elvis, Pat Boone, and the Rolling Stones. That's Dee Dee. Dee Dee, then a thin—actually skinny in high school—tall African American high school student who was spirited, smart, and just straight up fun. Today? Well, some things never change.

Famous Mae and Dee Dee story. During our senior year we were in the same English class, taught by my homeroom teacher of four years, Mrs. Roberts. Mrs. Roberts and I had been mutual admirers for all that time. For example, I was the first girl ever to sign up for drafting class at Morgan Park, and Mr. Okelpek, the drafting teacher came to ask her about me. Mrs. Roberts assured him I was sincere. Mr. Okelpek learned that I wanted to be an engineer and he made sure I learned a lot about engineering drawings. He was pretty cool, too.

I only lived a couple blocks from school, but I was occasionally late to class. In fact, I had several tardy slips. One morning, I passed Dee Dee in the hallway as she went to get a late slip. I thought, maybe, just maybe Mrs. Roberts will take pity on me. So I continued to class. Approximately one minute after the bell rang, I walked into the classroom. Mrs. Roberts smiled and told me to sit down. I took my assigned seat right in front of her desk, and class continued. We discussed the novel the class was currently reading. However, my neck began to tingle.

I felt dirty looks and arrows slung from the students sitting behind me. It was not especially different from the usual "goings on" in that class. I always did my homework and would "help the class out with the answers" whenever Mrs. Roberts asked me to. Was I an "apple polisher"? No, I don't think so. Yeah it was honors English and many other students just did not answer because it was Mrs. Roberts, and they didn't like her. But, hey, I did like her, and she was my homeroom teacher. You cannot antagonize everyone and survive to live long and prosper.

Anyway, Dee Dee walked into the classroom about two minutes after I did, handed Mrs. Roberts her tardy slip, glared at me and sat down. The intensity of the darts, arrows, and dirty looks flung in my direction intensified. What's the problem? I haven't answered any more questions or smiled more ingratiatingly than usual. *Y'all know me, I'm right there with you to mock Mr. Meade and Mr. O'Bannon.* But, to Mrs. Roberts I am goodness and light. You know I suck up to Mrs. Roberts; I can't alienate all the teachers. It was not my intent to. After all, Mrs. Branecki even made me a gym leader my junior year, instead of waiting for my senior year, even after I got a D in gym in freshman year.

Everyone confronted me after class. "I can't believe it." "Don't you have any dignity?" "You came in after Dee Dee."

"She made Dee Dee go get a tardy slip. She told you 'Welcome, Mae.'" I smiled sheepishly and said nothing.

I ask you, what should I have done? Volunteer to keep solidarity with Dee Dee, a fellow student, and get the fifth tardy slip that would require my parents to come up to school? Or go with the flow? Dee Dee, I rest my case.

Actually, I didn't get the most flack about the tardy slip and Mrs. Roberts from Dee Dee, but from Tony Green and Lynda Bundrage—my aces. The three of us hung out all the time, three of the most hip/"un-hip" people. I was student council president, Lynda was vice president and Tony was parliamentarian. And by the way, Mr. O'Bannon adored Lynda. Tony had a Datsun that he drove to school, so unless Lynda and I irritated him, we generally had wheels. Lynda was Miss Cutie Pie, always perfectly dressed, and coifed, and she tried to act grown up.

For some reason, Lynda and Tony thought they could sing. So they formed this group called "The Sands of Time" and convinced Dee Dee to join. Dee Dee had a great singing voice. I didn't feel left out because I knew I couldn't sing. It wasn't until I went to Tony's house to watch them practice that I found out that Lynda and Tony couldn't sing either. It was pitiful. But their costumes matched.

My high school career can be summarized by the following paradoxes. (If you don't know that word, look it up.)

1. I received the award for academic achievement in English instead of in science. The paradox was that I was not particularly known as an English maven, although I did get all As. Science was what I was known for, and I was the only student from my high school to consistently enter and win awards in science fairs, including city-wide science fairs. I scored very high on the math and physics SAT tests. I received scholarship offers from MIT, Rensselaer Polytechnic Institute, Bell Labs, as well as from Stanford. And yes, I got all As in science as well.

2. After being voted "Most Popular" and "Most Likely to Succeed," I had a post-graduation barbecue with the girl voted "Sexiest" (Lynda Bundrage) and my male "Most Popular" counterpart (Tony Green) but no one came. We sent out invitations weeks in advance. On the other hand, my sister Ada Sue held a small party announced on a day she was not at school, and our house was so crowded with invitees and crashers that folks were angry when they were turned away.

A LAST BREATH OF ADOLESCENCE

"Okay, Mother, please let me go. I'll be going off to college in a month anyway. It'll be me, Lynda, Tony, Tony's little cousin, and his grandparents. It'll be safe. Please?"

"I don't know."

"Please say, 'Yes!'"

"Okay, but just for the weekend."

"So, you all, I can go to Idlewild, Michigan. But Tony you know how to keep your cousin away from me. I do not like little, bad, noisy kids."

That's what the summer after finishing high school and that dud graduation party was like. Tony, Lynda, and me, hanging out. I had a summer job. I helped the Morgan Park administrator in the Pupil Employment Program sponsored by the Mayor's Office of the City of Chicago. By the time the summer program came to an end, I was responsible for submitting the payroll, keeping attendance, and finding placements for the other students. During the day, I learned how to persuaded businesses to hire students, I verified if there were really jobs at their locations, tattled on poorly performing placement sites to the director, and calculated hours and salaries.

In the evening Tony, Lynda, and I would frequently go to the drive-in movies. We were not particularly good drive-in movie neighbors. Yes, we did disturb the folks in the cars next to us with our continuous commentary on the action, heroine, hero, implausibility of the plot, coolness, etc. Come on, with movies like *The Mack, Coffy,* and the *Tales from Crypt,* you gotta talk. Sometimes folks in the neighboring cars became irritated with us, like the time I said "I'm gonna close my eyes" during a scary film, and a *BIG* woman in the car next to me said, "I wish you would close your mouth." Or, there was the time we had to move the car to another space and sneak to the concession stand because the guy in the car next to us threatened to kick Tony's butt if he didn't stop talking. Tony with his "no fighting self" then lipped off. We had to make a fast relocation.

Back to Idlewild. Idlewild, Michigan, was where the Three Musketeers, as we deemed ourselves, were going to spend one last fun filled three-day weekend. We would soon be going our separate ways. Tony to Hampton Institute in Virginia, Lynda to Spelman College in Atlanta, and me to Stanford University in Palo Alto, California. We were all changing, even then.

Here was the proposition: Tony's grandparents had a house in the country. A county fair was scheduled there over the weekend. All we had to do was to pick up Tony's disorderly little cousin Daryl and drive up in Tony's grandparents' car. (Not his trademark green Datsun. By the way, Tony owned a lot of green stuff, as his name was Tony Green. Childish?

Square? Yes, but it worked for him.) Simple enough plan if Daryl was kept away from me and Lynda didn't act too prissy while we were in the woods.

Great first step. We all made it to Michigan. I hadn't put Daryl out on a strip of lonely highway 50 miles outside of Chicago. We lugged Lynda's enormous suitcase full of new, cute clothes and deposited it in the house. Tony and I grabbed our small bags. We went to our rooms and since it was night time and pitch-black outside, we went to sleep.

Bright and early the following morning we took Tony's grandparents' car and went into town after eating breakfast. The carnival was in full swing with rides, gaming booths, cotton candy, and homemade ice cream. Tony and I ate until we were sick. We waited in line for this ride called the Hammer, which had two large cages on the end of large struts that just swung around a pivot point. During the ride, scared silly, we screamed, and generally embarrassed ourselves. Upon exiting the Hammer, Tony and I looked at each other, terror and tears in our eyes, and said, "Gotta go again." Back in line we went.

All day, Lynda hung away from us, a bit aloof. We noticed that she didn't laugh at our jokes as much. She didn't appreciate it when we goosed her. Lynda seemed to be getting all stuffy and prissy in preparation to go to a sophisticated all-women's college. (I still couldn't believe she was going to an all girls' school.)

Tony and I kept behaving childishly and having lots of fun. He commented on Lynda wearing a chic pair of large sunglasses. She was acting particular, proper and very adult, like the sophisticated twin on *The Patty Duke Show*. So that's what Tony called her: "Patty Duke."

Needless to say, Lynda didn't appreciate it. By dusk, we were exhausted, and broke, and had teased Lynda until she was extremely irritated with us. So we all climbed into the car to go home. I offered Miss Duke the front seat with Tony. But she'd had enough of both of us and jumped into the back. Just as Tony was starting up the car, a spider scurried across the back seat. Lynda screamed bloody murder and asked us to kill it. Tony howled with laughter. I said, "That little spider can't do anything to a great big old you." Patty Duke commanded that we kill it, *now*. I said, "Oh no, not me." Tony smiled and said it was getting closer. Lynda replied, "Oh, I wish you two would just grow up." Unfortunately for Lynda, we did not grow up that weekend, and the spider stayed alive and seated comfortably next to her. That fact made Tony's and my day. Of course, we had to grow up later.

But not just yet. That night, while sitting around the kitchen table just hanging out chatting, Tony and I got into some kind of nonsensical disagreement. So I decided to toss the little water left in my glass on Tony's face. He tossed the water in the pitcher onto my face. We were both laughing. Lynda scooted back from the table smirking and declared herself "not involved" as Tony casually walked over to the sink, presumably to get some dish towels … he ran water in a pot. He promptly poured the water on Patty Duke's head. A full-fledged water fight ensued as sophistication took a time-out.

THERE'S A CHANGE IN THE AIR

BOYS / CRUSHES

Leroy. Leroy was the first real boy that I *liked*. I don't even remember Leroy's last name, but I had a big crush on him, and I think he liked me, too. I met him in fourth-grade summer school. I can remember much of it vividly. He was brown-skinned with a short haircut. He was quite cute, and all the girls liked him. We were about the same height. He was smart, too. *Almost* as smart as me. He may have even known some things I didn't, and he had nice legs.

Usually, Leroy went to Fermi Elementary School. He was attending my school, Alexander Dumas Elementary, just for summer school. We really didn't even live in the same neighborhood. He was the first and last boy for a long time that I didn't mind talking to. In fact, I liked talking to him and got butterflies in my stomach around him. He liked the fact that I had a natural hairstyle, when many of the other kids made fun of me since for girls, it was not cool to have short nappy hair. We worked on projects together and sat next to each other in class.

I only saw him one time after summer school. He walked over to my street. I saw him while I was playing jump rope after school one day. I was so excited to see him. If only I could just talk to him a little while, but I couldn't act too interested for two reasons. First, if Ada Sue and Ricky saw, I would never be able to live it down; second, I wasn't allowed to play with boys by myself.

Actually, I could not go out on an official date with a boy until I was 16 years old. I turned sixteen in October of my senior year in high school! So, while skipping seventh grade was great academically, and in some ways socially, too, there were some disadvantages that put me behind my classmates.

That's okay, because I didn't really start to *like* boys until I was fourteen anyway and again it happened at summer school. I almost always went to summer school, because I could not bear not being busy and I loved learning. This time I took chemistry at Kenwood High School in Hyde Park, the summer between my sophomore and junior year. I wanted to take as much science as I could, as soon as I could. I didn't want to wait until my senior year to take chemistry. That particular summer was memorable not only because I met TBH ("the Big Hunk"), but also because I repaid my brother big time for his stunts when I was younger. If I say so myself, it was one of my best moves. I'll chronicle it later.

Oh, it's too good, let me tell it now. As teenage siblings, Ricky and I were allies outside the house, but at home we had numerous ongoing conflicts from wearing one another's jeans or jackets without permission to cleaning the dog poop out of the yard to fighting over my blackmailing him regarding his classified, secret girlfriends. There was always tension between us. I really don't remember what got this particular battle started, but I successfully ended it.

Ricky really made me mad one night, and he got the last lick in. At seventeen, he was still bigger than I was, but I could give him a run for his money. This time I proposed if he didn't leave me alone, I would punch a hole in his waterbed. It was an idle threat and we both knew it. It was too destructive and would get me into serious trouble with the greater powers that be, my parents. Knowing that idle threats were self-defeating,

I had to think of something else, a substantive way to follow through. The solution came to me in the middle of the night. I knew how to execute it and make a clean getaway. I would carry out retribution as I walked out the door to catch the bus at seven in the morning. My father would still be home to block any brutal retaliations. After the long bus ride to Kenwood High School, I would be fifty blocks away. Ample distance would then separate me from Ricky.

Morning came and I dressed while Ricky snoozed. He always slept late. My mother and father, who were always up early to go to work, were already in the kitchen. I quietly put my books and bag by the door and unlocked it. My heart pounded rapidly in my chest. My arms felt watery and my stomach churned. Timing was everything. It would be close. I calmly walked into the kitchen and filled a large soup kettle with ice and water. I went to my father to get lunch money and to let him see that I was fully dressed and ready for school. The pieces of the plan were in place. Nothing was left but the execution.

I picked up my weapon and went quietly to Ricky's room. Flinging open the door, I called his name. Half-open eyes stared up at me from a deep sleep. Realization slowly dawned and Ricky's eyes bucked. He shouted, "Mae, you better not …" just as the ice-cold water, soup pot, and everything else splashed across his face and body, soaking his bed clothes.

He jumped out of bed quickly, but I was faster. I grabbed my books and bag and was out the door as I heard my father say, "Boy, you better leave that girl alone." *Sheer perfection.* I walked, skipped actually down the two sunlit blocks to the bus stop, to Kenwood, chemistry and TBH.

TBH was tall, muscular, and going into his senior year. He was in my chemistry class. He was the quarterback for our arch-rival football team, Chicago Vocational High School (CVS). My school, Morgan Park, was one of the few integrated public high schools in Chicago, and it was also considered to be a school where the goody two-shoes, college prep, and middle-class kids went. CVS on the other hand, had a reputation for having some tough kids. It was twice as big as Morgan Park back then. In fact, at the football games between the Morgan Park Mustangs and the CVS Cavaliers, Morgan Park students were always let out of the stadium first. This gave us a headstart to get on the bus, into cars, or just get some "hat"—get away as quickly as possible. This was particularly important if we won and chants of "Humbug, Humbug" after the game echoed from the other side of the stadium, our opponents challenging us to a fight. (I must add, just for pride's sake, that Morgan Park was not the biggest wimp in the Red

Division South High School football league. Actually, we used to chant "Humbug, Humbug" after the game to Bogan High School. Of course, we never did anything, but we were held, while they left early.)

As occasional lab partners that summer, I learned a lot about TBH and his pride for CVS. Contrary to my preconceptions concerning handsome, muscular football players, he was very intelligent, disciplined, and willing to follow my lead. Though you know, willing or not, I was going to take the lead in science class. I was impressed by the fact that he was very conscientious about measurements and by how he recorded his experimental results. I didn't feel compelled to check his work. In fact, he was possibly more meticulous than I was. No, I am not and was not obsessive, but I just wanted things to be correct. It was my lab grade, as well. TBH and I had discussions about all kinds of things. He lived with his mother and worked after school. He was a member of the ROTC.

Surprisingly, TBH liked me also. I say "surprisingly" because though I knew I had a face adults thought was pretty, I never really dressed up. I always wore pants. People occasionally still called me "son," because of my short hair. But it didn't bother me as I was having too much fun with ballet and modern dance classes, science fairs, plays, pom-pom girls, riding my bicycle, reading, harassing my brother, student politics, museums, whatever; besides there would be time for boys later. It even embarrassed me a bit to like boys. *Shhh*, I didn't want my parents to know. And definitely not my brother or sister, since I had made their dating lives miserable every chance I got, in that annoying little sister kind of way. TBH and I spent lots of time talking in class; occasionally we would take the same bus on the way home. But we never went on a date in high school. We exchanged phone numbers and addresses and stayed in contact. He went to the United States Naval Academy in Annapolis, Maryland. That was my first introduction to military academies. (At that time, the academies did not accept women, which I thought was bogus.) TBH and I continued to write to each other and kept abreast of one another's lives through college. We later went on a few dates while I was at Stanford.

That's it, no more stories, otherwise I will have to change names to protect the innocent, the guilty, the trifling, the wonderful, and those who don't know they were targeted but missed. I had my heart broken a few times, and I may have broken a few myself. But I am here, healthy and happy.

Here's my one "I'm older than you, I've been through this, just trust me" piece of advice. Take the high school and college romances with an appropriate grain of salt. Why? Because first, at that stage in life, very few people actually know what they want. Those who believe they do, often want something or someone that may not be right or beneficial for them. You are still learning not only about the world but also about yourself at a very fast pace; with any luck you will continue to learn things about yourself, your career, your likes and dislikes, and just plain new stuff. More likely than not, that boy or girl will not be the love of your life and probably will not be around in one or two years except, if you're lucky, as a friend. I know it's true—a few lucky couples do last and build a wonderful life together, and I personally know some—but it's not the norm. And finally, as an engineering classmate of mine noticed, boyfriends and girlfriends always, always seem to mess up in some way close to finals or important midterms. They're not malicious, it's probably just the stress.

Now, whether it's the star running back, the neurotic dropout, an engineering major, a political scientist, or an artist, I can say without going into details, without hesitation, from my experience and the experiences of my friends and classmates, male and female, these are good words of advice. Pay attention. I wish someone had given me a hint earlier.

ENCOUNTERS WITH THE SANTA ANA

MOVING TO "THE FARM"

I was nervous, excited, lonely, sad, and happy all at the same time. I was sixteen years old, standing in O'Hare Airport with my parents, waiting to board a plane for San Francisco, California. I was on my way to Stanford University by myself. I had never seen the campus. Neither I nor anyone in my immediate family had ever been to California before.

I was wearing a maroon wool shirt jacket that I had made, a turtleneck, and jeans. It was toward the end of September in Chicago and still fairly warm. My suitcase contained a number of outfits, mostly pants that I had diligently sewn during the previous two weeks. I made most of my own clothes back then. I could sew exactly what I wanted, and it was cheaper to buy good cloth and have well-made clothing than to purchase things from the stores. The trunk that I had mailed ahead to Stanford had all my heavy-duty items: an iron, new towels, blankets, black-and-white polka-dot sheets, a small black-and-white television set, boots, my coats and winter clothes, and the books I wanted with me.

My mother, father, and I had spent the last three weeks preparing for my college start. It felt like old hat because this was really our third time; we were all involved when my sister and brother had already gone off to university. But this time I was leaving. I spent most of the money I had made from summer work and local academic awards buying my college stuff. I was proud that I had been able to buy myself a TV and new gray Hush Puppies shoes. I still had about $200 of my own to take with me to open a checking account. I had never had a checking account before, but I was confident I could handle it because I had always watched my mother balance hers.

My mother looked sad. My father was stoic. I was determined not to cry after all I hadn't cried in over four years but I was leaving home. I had always looked forward to going away to school. This was something I had to go through in life. I was going to exactly the school I wanted. I was embarking on a career in engineering and would have teachers, rather professors, who would challenge me and mentor me in a science career. And I was going to California, the heart of new things and innovation, radical politics, and cool science. Stanford University, known as "The Farm," was the first university to have coed dorms with girls and boys on the same floor. I had read about it in *Esquire* magazine.

As boarding time came closer, I began to worry about my parents. What would they do without me? Could they cope? I would write often, but long distance calls were too expensive. I hoped my parents would not worry about me. I would be just fine. After all, I had grown up in a big city, and I was smart and healthy.

As the plane began its decent into the San Francisco Bay Area, I could see the Sierra Nevada Mountains and the foot-hills that led to the Pacific Ocean. It was a brilliant, clear day. The pilot said we would get wonderful views of the Bay Area as we were routed along the peninsula. "Ladies and gentlemen, on the left of the plane all those red tile roofs are Stanford University." It came over the speaker. I was actually here. My heart skipped, and a big smile came to my face. *I'm here,* I thought.

The instructions on the freshman arrival form said there would be Stanford representatives with signs at baggage claim.

After collecting my bags and identifying myself to the Stanford folks, I was directed to the location to wait for the Stanford bus. I leaned on the wall—cool, relaxed, and in control, at least that's the appearance I wanted to give. A young man came up and introduced himself as a member of the Stanford Black Student Union (BSU). The BSU was helping to welcome the African American students and transport them to campus. So I got in the van with a number of other students. The drive down the 101 expressway, which I learned was called a "freeway" in California, was filled with talk about what to expect and what events the BSU was putting on to welcome students. Quite a few of the students were living in Roble Hall, the Black Theme House dormitory. I was not.

The bus entered Stanford's grounds via Palm Drive. The campus was beautiful. Trees, palms, plants, and flowers were everywhere. The air was fresh. The stone and stucco buildings were golden beige with red tile roofs. The van dropped me off in the parking lot of the Florence Moore Hall dormitory. There was a table set up in the parking lot. As I looked around trying to figure out what to do, I heard my name. "Mae." *Not possible*, I thought, *I do not know anyone here.* Again, "Mae! Up here."

I looked up and saw this young blonde woman leaning

out of a window of the second floor, waving. "I'm Janet, your roommate." Janet Waggoner was probably the best roommate I could have had that year. She was 5'10" or 5'11" tall. I was not used to women taller than me. She was nineteen and had spent a year in Sweden as an exchange student. Janet grew up in Oakdale, California, on a ranch in the San Joaquin Valley. She was from a small rural town; I was from the big city. She had a great smile and a sunny personality.

I was a bit overwhelmed that Janet had been on the lookout for me. She had recognized me from the pictures of students posted on our Alondra House dorm bulletin board. She came downstairs and helped me with my bags. We lugged my trunk up the stairs. Then we settled down and talked. She knew all about Stanford. I just knew it had a good engineering school and football team and a bit about the academics. Over the year, Janet and I studied together under the shadow of the Stanford radio telescope dish in the foothills behind campus. We pooled our resources and cooked our meals together when the campus food service workers went on strike spring quarter. I even learned to ride and groom horses at her family's ranch.

Alondra was a four-class coed dorm. It not only had freshmen, but also sophomores, juniors, and seniors. But right then, the only upperclassmen present were our resident assistants, Tammy and John. They got all the freshman together that evening, about ten to twelve of us, to brief us on freshman orientation. Tammy was a junior and pre-med student from Southern California and reminded me of the real-life version of the Beach Boys song refrain, "I wish they all could be California girls." She also drove a Mercedes, which her parents replaced with an Audi when "The Benz" had mechanical problems. John was a senior pre-med major from Philadelphia. He was intense and funny.

People already knew a lot about each other including me. They knew I intended to be an engineering major and that I was only sixteen and the youngest person in the dorm. That fact provided endless entertainment throughout the year, but not in a mean-spirited way. For example, when I got a traffic ticket, I had to get an adult, someone over eighteen, to go with me to juvenile court since my parents were in Chicago. Ha ha. My dorm mates thought it was pretty cool that I was so young and in college, but they never treated me any differently.

In our group, we had folks from all over the United States, from the East Coast to Birmingham, Alabama, to small towns in Kansas, and, of course, throughout California. We were all excited to be at Stanford.

Linda Jones, also an African American freshman from Chicago, lived in Alondra. She played tennis (really well), spoke French, had been to Europe, and loved to dance. Her father, a pediatrician, and her mother came to California with Linda to help her settle in. Linda and I became great friends. Later, as anchorwoman on the Houston evening news, Linda covered my launch to space. True story.

I found camaraderie and support in the dorm. I took part in school activities and dorm shenanigans. One really cool thing was playing intramural football. Did I forget to tell you the real reason I wanted to go to Stanford? Football. I was a football fanatic. Stanford played what was termed "Razzle-Dazzle" football. You know—punt and field goal fakes, lateral-lateral passes. Stanford had won the Rose Bowl two years in a row before I arrived. Once they denied their Big Ten Rose Bowl opponent a touchdown or field goal with first down on the one-yard line. The football team, the band, and the fans were fun. The four linebackers were called the "Thunder Chickens" because they were smaller than a lot of other college football line backers. Anyway, Stanford football was a big draw for me, *and* they had coed intramural football leagues.

I had never actually played football before. I knew the plays and strategies, but I had never played. I was athletic and strong and roughhoused with my brother, so I was definitely game to be on our dorm football team. However, I mistakenly thought that to block in touch football, you merely had to get in the way of the opponent, not really *tackle* them. The Alondra dorm team consisted of two girls (Tammy and me) and regular guys (read normal-sized, not particularly imposing males), and our first game was against a fraternity team (read big and mean). That game taught me several things. First, the only time just "touching" counts as a tackle is with the person carrying the ball, otherwise you get bumped. Second, some guys will try to intimidate women with their strength. Third, and most importantly, it feels good to make a good, solid hard block. Especially "hitting" a big guy who thought he had you intimidated and thought a girl couldn't stop him. That's fun. During my intramural football career, I sustained the only broken bone I ever had in my life, a hairline fracture of my left index finger when I almost caught a "long bomb." It hurt like crazy, but I kept playing. This was too much fun!

BEING WHAT I INTENDED TO BE

My Leland Stanford, Jr. University Diploma of Graduation reads, "*Conferred on Mae Carol Jemison, who has satisfactorily pursued the studies and passed the examinations required, therefore the Degree of Bachelor of Science with all the rights, privileges and Honors there unto appertaining …*" My diploma was signed by the chair of the Chemical Engineering Department and the Dean of the School of Engineering. My formal transcript from Stanford lists my degree as BS Chemical Engineering, and notes *"Also fulfilled the requirements for an BA in African and Afro-American Studies."* Stanford at that time did not grant two degrees unless you spent an extra year in residence. I completed the course requirements for both Chemical Engineering and African and Afro-American Studies in four years.

The reason why I completed two degrees in four years permeates my journey at Stanford. Actually, it reveals obstacles placed purposefully or accidentally in my path to achieve something others may not have believed I could or should accomplish and the measures I took to become the person I intended to be.

I arrived at Stanford with the intention of doing an interdepartmental major in biomedical engineering, a new field that I had learned about during a two-week program sponsored by the Junior Engineering Technical Society (JETS) at the University of Illinois in Urbana. I had attended the JETS program prior to my senior year in high school. That summer I was able to reconcile my love of physics, biology, practical implementation, and creativity in this one area of biomedical engineering. When I considered colleges to attend, actually I didn't just look at football teams, but also the engineering schools and interdisciplinary-major possibilities. Being politically and socially aware, I also considered other curricula and benefits offered by the university: Dr. Linus Pauling; the mile-long Stanford Linear Accelerator Center; the radio telescopes on campus; its great engineering, medical, law and business schools; its location in California; and its great football team. Stanford University was clearly the hands-down winner.

My goals my first quarter at college were: to find an academic advisor in biomedical engineering; to continue gaining fluency in Russian, which I was convinced would be important in science and space exploration; to become involved in dance and athletics; and to do well in my classes. I had always gotten along well with and been supported by my teachers. I had gone to an integrated high school and had scored high on the standard academic tests, the ACT and SAT, including the physics and math specialty exams. I had received scholarship offers not only from all the schools I had applied to, including Massachusetts Institute of Technology, Cornell, and Rensselaer Polytechnic Institute, but also from their alumni associations, as well. I was confident and outgoing and worked really hard, but I was unprepared for the response I got from my engineering advisor.

Advisees were invited over to Dr. Kline's house. I had never been in one of my teacher's homes before. It was a bit intimidating to be there. I do not remember exactly how many advisees he had, but I do remember I was the only young black woman. Everyone seemed at ease and friendly. No one spoke to me much, but I tried to join in. People were discussing their schedules, what courses they should take, and what courses they tested in or out of.

I had taken four years of Russian in high school, and I was pretty good at it, so I took the Russian placement test. The test and instructions were in Russian, which by the way, has a different alphabet from English. After the test we were told that our advisors would let us know what class to sign up for.

In high school I had also taken solid analytic geometry and calculus. So trying to join in and be casual like everyone else, I asked my advisor if I should take the accelerated calculus without solid analytic geometry, since I had already had it. He said no, just take the regular calculus for engineering, physics, and math majors. I was a bit surprised that he said this without discussing my background in mathematics. Later that evening I was devastated when I asked how to find out what class to take in Russian. Dr. Kline said, and I remember clearly, "If they have not contacted you, just assume that you should take beginning Russian." I wanted to cry. For the first time in my academic career, here was a teacher, a professor, who was supposed to help me, telling me twice in one evening that

I had learned little in high school. He doubted me without bothering to learn anything about me. I worried that, I must really not be as bright as everyone was telling me and as my scores seemed to reflect, if after four years I could not place out of first-quarter Russian.

As silly as it may seem now, and as silly as it seemed to me my junior year at Stanford, I was actually too embarrassed to go to the Russian Language Department to find the real answer. I was too embarrassed to let them know I had taken four years of Russian, but still might be in the beginning class. Consequently, I never took Russian at Stanford.

When I started at Stanford, I had a very easy smile. In fact, I smiled and was so optimistic, that I remember one senior, Vivian, a gorgeous Black woman with short natural hair called me "Smiley." Though she was not a science major, she cautioned me not to take too seriously what some folks would say about my intended course of study in engineering. For example, one African American pre-med junior called "Wild Bill" advised me that no African Americans had passed Calculus 41A the first time. I did not take his advice to heart, but began to realize that if I was to make it in engineering, I would probably have to make it on my own.

There were other African American students majoring

in engineering my year and in the classes ahead of me, but I didn't meet them and the Black graduate students until much later. Though we all may not have been in the same classes, they were a tremendous help navigating the waters. My first quarter classes consisted of calculus and solid analytic geometry, introductory chemistry, freshman seminar on women's physiology, freshman English focused on African American literature, and tennis.

I had always been very good in science. I was *so* looking forward to my chemistry class. I sat right up front in the lecture hall so I could hear everything. I was eager. Some of the folks at the dorm advised me that the professor I had for chemistry was a bit of a jerk and was not interested in students. But I took the section anyway because it fit in well in my schedule. The subject matter was fascinating. We were learning about the Schrödinger equation. I was "geeked." But when I would ask questions, Professor Weinhardt would either ignore me or act as though I was impossibly dumb for not knowing the answer. When a white boy down the row asked the exact same questions, Weinhardt would say, "Very good observation," and explain. I gradually stopped asking questions; in fact, I became too timid to ask anything. I drifted to the back row of the lecture hall.

By winter quarter my first year, I had a new engineering advisor from the Chemical Engineering Department, Dr. Channing Robertson whose specialty was biomedical engineering. He advised me to be a chemical engineering major because I'd earn a classical degree. Everyone would know that I had completed a rigorous program of study, something they wouldn't be able to tell from an interdepartmental major. Anyway, Dr. Roberts said by the time I completed the course work he would approve for my biomedical engineering interdisciplinary major, I would be only a few courses shy of being a chemical engineer. He was a good, caring, convincing advisor, and I settled into the chemical engineering track.

I also wanted to take some language courses. My mother and father had always impressed upon me the importance of being well-rounded. Still embarrassed about Russian, I took Swahili. I thought, Swahili, where else would I learn it? My sister Ada Sue had taken a year of Swahili in college. At Stanford Swahili was taught out of the Linguistics Department. The course was extraordinarily interesting. The linguistics professor approached teaching this language by discussing its historical basis and phonetic structure. For example, Swahili has no gender, but classifies object words according to the object's use and philosophical categorization. And even more important, the professor was interested in me.

My freshman year I also found African and modern dance classes, acted in the play "No Place to Be Somebody," and was in the musical "Purlie." I was starting to get into the flow of school and social life.

Bell Labs wanted to increase the numbers of minority and women students engaged in engineering and the sciences. I had a National Achievement Scholarship, sponsored by Bell Labs. One of the benefits, besides scholarship money, was that Bell Labs would employ its scholarship recipients during the summer. My experience at Bell Labs during my freshman summer gave me a respite from the struggle to be accepted by many in the science and engineering faculties at Stanford. That summer I worked at Bell Laboratories in Naperville, Illinois. I learned the computer language PL/1 and refreshed the FORTRAN IV programming skills I had learned in high school. I wrote computer programs that were used throughout the center. I read and documented existing programs, learned to troubleshoot computer systems, and even occasionally was compelled to look through some BASIC and machine language code for bugs. I worked with two young white males, full-time programmers who were impressed with all the work I did in such a short time.

Never a wallflower, I started asserting myself more my second year. Sophomore year I took a political science class on Politics in Sub-Saharan Africa. It was taught by Professor David Abernathy, who was supposed to be one of the toughest political science professors at Stanford. The course was wonderful. Professor Abernathy demanded that we read lots of books and analyze the information. He enjoyed my participation in his class, even though I was not a political science or social science major.

I continued to dance. I was elected Black Student Union president. I kept up with Janet and my friends from my freshman dormitory, though I now lived in Lagunita Court the new Black Theme House dormitory.

Over the four years, my career at Stanford was marked by many extracurricular activities and student leadership. I designed and helped teach two classes at Stanford, one called Race and Politics in Education and the other, Race and Culture in the Caribbean. I became more and more interested in the history, politics, languages, and cultures of Africa. I continued to take Swahili classes just because I liked them. I took more political science and history courses on Africa and continued to take dance classes. I even drove with Linda Jones and other friends to Oakland to take African dance classes at Everybody's Creative Arts Center. All the while, I doggedly pursued my major in chemical engineering, I also took classes of interest in the sciences and engineering like Life Sciences in Space Exploration, Biomedical Instrumentation, and Biomedical Fluid Mechanics (simultaneously with my first fluid mechanics course). All were graduate school courses, but hey, this was information I wanted to learn. The professors seemed pleased that I found their courses of interest and gave me permission to attend. I rose to the occasion and did well.

Summers I worked at Bell Labs on printed wiring for materials and on nuclear magnetic resonance spectroscopy.

During the spring quarter of my junior year while counting up course credits, I found I was just two required courses shy of fulfilling the requirements for a major in African and Afro-American studies. I was on track for completing chemical engineering, as I had intended. Why had I taken so many of these political science, history, culture, and linguistics classes? I had just planned to be a science and engineering person. Certainly, chemical engineering, which had the most course requirements of any Stanford major, had kept me busy. So had my extra-curricular activities and on again/off again social life.

I took the courses because they interested me, and I realized even then, that the professors in those classes wanted me there. I felt they believed in me as a student, unlike the feeling I got in most of the engineering and science classes. I did not have to jump over extra hurdles each time I walked in the door just to prove I belonged there. The social sciences professors were interested in my ideas, insights, and comments. My intelligence was legitimate and welcomed. Looking back, I realize that it had been important for me as a student to have professors who believed in me, teachers who felt that I could be one of their colleagues. I majored in African and Afro-American studies because I was unconsciously balancing the poor reception I often received in the science and engineering programs with the warm embrace of political science.

I was probably a much better physical scientist than I was a social or political scientist, although my academic grades do not reflect that. But academically at Stanford, I could not afford to relinquish my heart, energy, and soul completely to the physical sciences because the majority of the professors pushed me away. Certainly, I ran into some helpful instructors like the Physics Department Chair who gave me an incredibly glowing recommendation for medical school and called me one of the most outstanding students he had met in his twenty-five years of teaching. He wondered why I did not major in physics. One organic chemistry professor called me into his office after one of my test scores was wildly variant (lower) from previous ones. We talked chemistry and he gave me an oral quiz. He suggested I become a chemistry major instead of an engineering major because they really needed bright students like me. I stuck with chemical engineering, however, because I was determined to do biomedical engineering.

People ask me what was the most difficult thing about majoring in engineering: being a woman, being black, or coming from public schools? I do not know. To finish engineering in four years, I had to adopt a "hunkered down" type of mentality. No matter what, I was going to complete engineering. I was determined to keep my sense of self, but it was bruised and bloodied. My self-confidence was intact and pulled me through; the self-confidence that I had built as a child and teenager by falling down and getting back up and knowing I was worthwhile just because I was me.

I want to be clear that I believe my reception by the science and engineering faculty would have been the same if not worse at any other prestigious, predominantly white university in 1973. I consider it my good fortune to have been at Stanford where I had other outlets for my talents and where there were some professors who were not completely close-minded.

The bad part of going off to school at 16 was that I did not know some of the professors' sexism and racism could be so great as to be threatened by the presence of someone unlike them. I was unprepared for the assault on and the disregard of my capabilities. Clearly, I had had prior run-ins, epic disagreements with teachers and authority figures, Black, white, male, and female. But, never had the people I looked up to and depended on for training doubted my intelligence and aptitude on sight. It was a harsh blow.

The good part of entering this environment at 16 was that I was still just brazen, arrogant, and unsocialized enough to find ways around these obstacles. At 16 and 17, I was still actively, aggressively exploring and pushing any limitation I came upon. And so, though it hurt to have folks doubt me, I just didn't care enough about convention or expected standards of behavior to bow to their concepts of me and their wishes that I would just disappear. I had no intention of doing so.

Dance was always very important to me and I believe helped me through Stanford. I think it is the creativity, athleticisim, musicality, and story narrative that must be integrated and communicated at the same time that makes dancing so invigorating and peaceful.

I loved all types of dance. At Stanford I took modern, jive and swing, Haitian, Brazilian and African dance. I performed in and choreographed dance productions, including some at the Palo Alto Community Theater.

The last quarter of my senior year, in addition to finishing the coursework for my Chemical Engineering and African Studies degrees, I decided to choreograph and stage a dance production. Yes, a full-fledged dance program in the Little Theater, with lights costumes and an intermission. I was inspired by Alvin Alley, the Dance Theater of Harlem, my dance instructor at Stanford Halifu Osumare and life. With a lot of help from my friend Billie Freeman, who was a freshman, I was able to pull off a really good production. That caused me to ponder the question that had been floating in my mind for more than a year. Should I go to NYC to become a professional dancer?

I worked out what I thought was a brilliant plan. I would request a year deferment from the medical school of my choice. Then I'd take a year off to see if I had what it took to make it as a professional dancer or choreographer. I'd support myself by doing part-time lab work—after all, I would have a ChemE degree from one of the best schools in the world and lots of lab experience. Sounds like a good plan, right?

That was until it was filtered through the sage lens of my mother. During our very frank and at time heated discussions, one concept broke through. My science career was more important to me than dance. As my mother said, *"You can always dance if you are a doctor. But you can't easily doctor if you are a dancer."*

I had friends with whom I laughed and played. I had out-lets for energy, enthusiasm, and frustration. I found small but consistent ways to maintain my sense of self and continue to build my self-confidence. I found ways to let the wind swirl around me and to open my wings and soar on its currents.

WIND CURRENTS

The World at Large, What It Was Telling Me,
and What I Heard On the Wind

ROLE MODELS AND IMAGES

Growing up, I pretended to be Honey West, the female private eye in the eponymously named in television series who had an ocelot. I liked that Honey West was in control and did not run to men or anyone else to save her. She saved all of them. Then there was the villainous Catwoman on *Batman*, played by Eartha Kitt. Catwoman did not always win, but I was captivated by her athleticism, sensuality, and daring. Oh yeah, the comic books. I liked Wonder Woman, one of the good guys, and Medusa, an evil woman, because they were drawn with muscles and were strong. I was not crazy about Sue Storm, the Invisible Girl with telekinetic powers, a member of the Fantastic Four, because she was always whining and crying up under her husband Reed Richards, Mr. Fantastic. I preferred to be like their nemesis, the Silver Surfer, part of the cosmos. When I was 5, 6, 7, and 8 years old and my brother, sister, and I played Flash Gordon, they always made me be Ming the Merciless. I was not adverse to being the villain. I tried to be cool and unemotional like Mr. Spock in *Star Trek*. Lt. Uhura was all technical competence and grace

I had my hair cut into a short, natural hairstyle like Miriam Makeba in fourth grade. In high school, I discovered Judith Jamison, the tall regal woman who was the star of the Alvin Ailey Dance Theater. That was a wonderful discovery, because already 5'7" tall as a sophomore in high school, I was tall for most women dancers.

Dr. Linus Pauling was great. He was a scientist who won a Nobel Prize in biochemistry and a Nobel Peace Prize for his work on trying to stop the atmospheric testing of nuclear weapons.

In college, I studied Julius Nyerere, the first president of the East African country of Tanzania, and how he had worked to keep Tanzania politically non-aligned with either the United States or the Soviet Union. He wanted Tanzanians to determine their own path after colonialism. In medical school, I read of the handsome, charismatic Che Guevara, a young physician born into a world of privilege, who tried to change the governance and policies of his country. He became a key revolutionary figure in Latin America. Che died violently at the age of thirty-nine. Isaac Asimov wrote with incredible clarity about worlds, peoples, and technologies that existed only in his imagination. Arnold Schwarzenegger parlayed his muscled physique beyond a strong man statue into a new genre of action films. In 1976, Shirley Chisholm declared her candidacy for the Democratic Party nomination for President of the United States. Shirley Bassey sang the theme to the James Bond movie *Goldfinger* and every other song that had the good fortune to be chosen by her with all the passion, understanding, and melody that is possible. Lola Falana danced. Gloria Steinem, while a journalist, posed as a Playboy Bunny and exposed the objectification of women, bringing attention to the fact that a new view of women was needed and that feminism was real.

I never met most of these people, fictional or real, but each one was an image of what may be possible in this world. As public figures, they were images that gave life to specific qualities and characteristics. I did not know what personal trials or tribulations they went through or how they managed to cope and excel in difficult times. But the results were impressive. They stood as testimony to the possible.

Each of these individuals and characters are among many who have affected me, some more strongly than others. Yet, they were not my role models because I did not know them or interact with them day-to-day. I did not know what they did when things didn't go as planned, or if they brushed their teeth every night. How did they treat their husbands or wives? How did they treat their cats? People less fortunate than them? Did they work late into the night to finish a project? Did they sacrifice some of themselves for others or only do things for their self-aggrandizement?

The types of skills and behaviors I used to see myself through the day I learned from the people whom I lived and interacted with every day: my mother and father, siblings, teachers, uncles and aunts, next-door neighbors, and friends. These people were my role models.

By encouraging me to look things up in the dictionary, even when I was not sure how to spell the word, my mother taught me the importance of research and self-reliance. Seeing my mother go back to school to get her teaching degree, and later a master's degree, while raising three children was an enduring lesson in perseverance and lifelong learning. She was always exploring all different subjects; reading books, newspapers, and magazines; and keeping abreast of current events.

I learned grooming, how to care for my skin, and how to put on make-up from my mother, by watching her get dressed for work each day. I remember she would sew us new outfits for special occasions, working through the night if need be.

My father's support of my mother's ambition dispelled prevailing social notions that a man must be in the foreground at all times. He worked while my mother finished college. I learned from my father that men could and should be responsible for fixing their own food and watching the children. He plaited my hair and got me ready for school. He and his friends would take me fishing and hunting. He taught me how to paint trim and "cut in" using the edge of the brush. When I was seven, eight, nine years old, I started to master the card game Bid Whist and its art of verbal one-upmanship with these men who appreciated and bragged about my assertiveness, my ability to count cards in my head, my will, daring, and sharp wit. I learned the ethics of responsibility observing my father work two jobs.

My uncle Louis talked with me about Einstein's theory of relativity and the size and distance of stars when I was nine and I learned then that I should and could understand anything. When my Aunt Melvyn selflessly gave of her time on weekends and when she let me go to the dry cleaner with her and work, I learned how hard folks work daily and also how to diligently press clothes well, how to share with others, and the importance of family.

My siblings taught me how to study and get good grades in school, as well as how to play chess, be cool, avoid parental wrath, and have fun. Ricky, Ada Sue, and I would stand up for one another, fall asleep on one another's laps, and forget the day's skirmishes. They would rock me to sleep when I was sick. Ada Sue held my hand as we crossed the street and would let me go on dates with her. I learned how to apply to college and medical schools to get scholarships from watching Ada Sue. Ricky took drafting classes which he did exceedingly well in and I learned what it was used for when he shared his experiences. My parents' patience with my science projects, that I always had to ask "why?" helped me incorporate tolerance of a little bit of chaos for a later good into my personality. These people, these role models, were the ones who made the biggest difference in my life.

Cats. All kinds of cats—from large Bengal tigers and super fast cheetahs to smallest rusty spotted cat of the forest and grasslands of India and Sri Lanka to the extinct sabre tooth tiger—they all fascinate me. And I am particularly intrigued by Felis catus or what we may call or think of as domesticated cats (whether they really are domesticated or not).

Since I can remember, I have wished to be like cats; to be able to co-opt some of their superpowers as my own. Cats are fast, stealthy, patient, confident, intelligent, self-sufficient, beautiful, flexible, curious, adventurous, cautious, with acute senses and self-determining.

Growing up I had always tried to imagine what it would be like to be able to hear, smell, see, and perceive the world as well as cats can. So I would try to push my senses to their limit. Could I know what's happening just by listening? I would push to see and operate in the dark, challenging my capacity to balance my body on anything that would substitute as a tight rope. Later, I would channel cats' ability to be social and friendly in groups *and* then walk away and explore completely alone.

Once, during a discussion group hosted by a major magazine in New York City, I had an epiphany when professor and actress Anna Deveare Smith stated that we don't just have to learn from humans—we can learn from everything around us if we open ourselves. That's when I realized that cats have always been major role models in my life. And I continue to gain skills, capabilities, and perspectives from them.

WAFTS OF FORMALDEHYDE
Medical School

HOW I REALLY LEARNED TO STUDY

It was not until medical school that I truly learned how to study and be a full-time, focused student. Not that academics and chemical engineering at Stanford had not been challenging. I had certainly done my full share of engineering problem sets, studied for tests, and spent lots of time in the library researching term papers—in high school and definitely in college. I always turned in my homework, usually on time. It's just that medical school demanded that you study every day *after* being in class from 9 a.m. to 5 p.m! No matter how bright you were, how quick on the uptake, you still had to study.

There were *volumes* of information that I had to commit to memory. There was no grading on the curve, no "A" for effort or "A" just because you answered fewer questions wrong than most other people. There was an absolute minimum amount of information you had to know, and know correctly, not "sorta" know. Think about it: Do you want your physician to "sorta" know where the major blood vessels in your arm are? Or "sorta" have an idea of how much medication to give in the middle of an emergency? Or only be able to prescribe one type of antibiotic because she hadn't bothered to learn about the others? Or, better still, say, "Wait, hold this bandage on your cut while I look up what vessel may be punctured. I'll be right back. Now, try not to bleed too fast."

It's all obvious to me now, but it was not when I arrived at Cornell University Medical College (CUMC) on 69th Street and York Avenue in New York City. My first priority in the selecting a medical school was to be in New York, that's where I wanted to live. Cornell was one of the best medical schools in the country. It had great student housing and good financial aid. It was on the East Side of Manhattan, in one of the best areas of the city. I was very pleased when I arrived in New York City just a week out of sunny California. I'd spent the summer after graduating from Stanford, working as an engineer at IBM in San Jose, driving my new black Camaro, and hanging out with a nutrition major from the University of California at Berkeley, a fellow Libran who called himself Mwalimu.

It took a week to drive the Camaro from California to Chicago where I left it with my mother. Though I had paid for the car with money I had made tutoring at Stanford, the provisions of my financial aid package to Cornell stipulated no cars. I understood. Why should they pay for you to spend more than $200 per month to a park?

"'NUFF SAID!"

Four years of growing up in California had molded me in certain ways, so I stepped out of the cab in front of Cornell's Olin Hall with a nice sunshine smile on my face. Californians, I found out later were considered a bit "soft" by folks in New York—and we dressed differently. Remember this was 1977, and all the things we accept now were not the norm. In fact, the age of "profiling" in nightclubs—you know, folks standing around dressed fabulously, trying to look good—was moving into full swing. People described by the terms "yuppies" and "buppies" were entering the workforce. Though under it all, I was really a Chicagoan, I had a lot of Californian tendencies and wore the garb.

Twenty years old, 5'9," 136 pounds, and muscular, I entered

Olin Hall dressed in tight faded blue jeans with holes in the knees and a few other places, a denim work shirt tied around my midriff, sandals, hair in a hundred small plaits all over my head, and two earrings in one ear and a feather in the other. I was armed with linear algebra, tons of differential and partial differential equations. I knew all about counter current flow and heat and mass transfer, and how to use Reynold's numbers in fluid flow equations. I could speak Swahili and knew quite a bit about the politics of Sub-Saharan and Southern Africa. I knew a little more anatomy than the average dancer does. And I thought pre-med students had a tendency to be overly obsessive-compulsive and never really delved into the fundamentals of scientific theory and process.

I had an easy smile, good political acumen, and a history of social activism, and I believed in myself. I could dance my fanny off. "*Nuff said.*" Oh yeah, I could play a diabolical hand of Bid Whist and I had bought a few new conservative outfits for fall.

I met my roommate, Joan Culpepper, an African American woman chemistry major from Smith College. We shared a bathroom between two adjoining rooms. Joan was cordial and friendly. I noticed she already had some anatomy books, and was reading through them. It was still two days before class started, so I pegged Joan as a *real* "pre-med." (You see, I wasn't a real pre-med because I had not decided to apply to medical school until spring quarter of my junior year in college. And I did not intend to practice medicine. In fact, one *real* pre-med friend at Stanford called me a *closet* "pre-med.") Still, Joan and I established an easy companionship that has lasted to this day. I learned later we had many things in common—she minored in Afro-American Studies and was into the arts and was a musician. I also found out that Joan always had "the scoop" about all things having to do with academics and medical school. From her, I learned that, including us, there were four Black women and six Black men in our class, 30 women, and 105 students total. Girlfriend had already scoped and purchased all the books for our classes and knew both upperclassman and professors.

While Joan and I were talking, there was a knock on my door. Standing there was this 6'4" brother who could have easily, in all truthfulness, given Arnold Schwarzenegger a run for his money. His name was Blaine Morton, and he had graduated with a degree in biochemistry from MIT. We all spoke "nice-nice" while establishing credentials. Blaine had grown up on Long Island. Joan had grown up in the Bronx and gone to the prestigious Bronx High School of Science. I was from Chicago. Next thing I knew, Blaine looked me up and down and said something about Chicagoans and "caps" on my plethora of plaits! *Oh, it's like that,* I thought. Since this was clearly and intimidation tactic, rather than getting into "signifying," or name-calling contest, I responded, "Blaine, don't make me kick your butt." Men are not used to women elevating the conversation to the physical so quickly, especially when they are big strapping fellows. Though I said it with a playful smile, Blaine didn't know if I was "kidding on the square." Joan just laughed as Blaine asked, "You're going to kick my butt?" My reply, "Right here, right now." With that skirmish settled, thereafter, Joan, Blaine and I became study partners. My introduction to the upperclassmen of the Cornell University Medical College community occurred later that evening at a social.

A get-together was held at Lasdon Apartments to welcome the upperclassman back and check out the first-year students. Still dressed in my California special travel outfit I walked with Joan to the high-rise building. There were about twenty Black people in the apartment, food, music and a "Rise 'n Fly" Bid Whist game. One of the guys suggested that the men play against the women. At some point, Joan and I sat down as partners. For those of you who don't know, Bid Whist is a game with levels of strategies, just like everything in life. Bets are made based on how many books of cards you think you can win, as in Bridge. If you make the number you bid or more, you receive the points. If you make fewer books than you bid, the entire bid is subtracted from your score. The first team to make seven points wins, or the first team to go minus seven, loses. There are of course many ways and strategies to win or force the other team to lose. If you lose, you and your partner have to get up and let another set of partners play.

The other critical component of a Bid Whist game is psychological intimidation, verbal one-upmanship, or "talking trash." How colorfully you can verbally express how well you played, how poorly the others played, or covering your mistakes (*not* the position to be in)? Subtle movements, including not saying anything and just "taking names," that is, winning, also work as intimidation techniques.

I was capable of trash talking with the best of them. But I believe etiquette demands that when you're new and trying to make a good impression, you should be mannerly. So, amid all the conversation, Joan and I just "took names." We won and were polite. The fact I had gone to college in California implied to the folks from the East Coast that I might be a bit of a pushover, so they didn't know not to try certain tactics. After Joan and I had caused multiple male groupings to rise and fly, one light-skinned brother from New York came in and asked, with a grin on his face, "How's it going? Are the girls losing?"

I tried y'all. I really did. I couldn't help it. I had been tired of being called a "girl" for a while. Black men would not tolerate been called anything with "boy" in it at all, so, why should I tolerate "girl?" I replied, "No, the women are winning, and the boys are losing." My first day at CUMC.

That night I took my plaits down, washed my hair, and got my conservative clothes out for the first day of medical school orientation and class. Orientation consisted of, if I remember anything about it all, someone telling us the schedule (many students already seemed to know it), giving us information about physical exams and vaccinations that we would get, and syllabi for classes were distributed. That's it.

GROSS ANATOMY

Our first class was Gross Anatomy, at 9 a.m. on Wednesday morning. In Gross Anatomy one learns about the muscles, internal organs, blood vessels, bones, and nerves. Basically, from my engineering point of view, these were the mechanical portions or the geography of the human body. I had seen Joan studying the dissection manual over the two days since I had arrived in New York—a clue I had ignored. I hadn't even bothered to buy my books yet. I sat in my seat shocked when after just 40 minutes of lecture hall discussion about the first dissection and a small commentary about where the cadavers or human bodies we were to dissect came from, we were given locker numbers, a group dissection number, told to change into our whitecoats and promptly report to the lab. My internal dialogue with myself and the world began.

Wait, wait, wait! Don't you want to give us a chance to adjust? Explain what you mean by "dissection," I've never cut a human cadaver. You mean the entire lab is filled with dead bodies? Who? Who goes first?

While I slowly walked into the lab, the formerly *real* premed students rushed in excitedly. When I arrived at my table, I met my cadaver partners. They, having been *real* pre-meds, were jockeying for position as to who would make the first incision. Not wanting to seem too out of it, the least I could do was stand close enough to see what they were doing, but no, I did not want to make the first incision or any other cut that day. Nor did I want to touch the cadaver. Didn't we need to wave some special talisman over her or something? (I found it was "a her," as the cadaver had one leg and one of my three lab partners quickly named her "Gams.")

Okay, everybody, just be cool. They haven't given us the special secrets. You know the secrets. The secrets that make it okay to cut someone open and look around inside. I am sure we need this information even if the body has been pickled in a large vat of form-

aldehyde for over a year, and the owner of it volunteered to donate it to medicine.

Ah, hell! Someone has already made a midline incision and is looking for the *what* muscle? Okay, the rectus abdominus.

I asked aloud, "May I see your dissection book?" To myself, I asked, "*What's an atlas?*" The dissection manual stated, "Identify the insertion of the rectus at the pubic symphysis." *The what?* One of my other cadaver mate says to look for the aponeurosis.

My instructions to myself: *Mae just keep looking at the dissection book.* It mentions that "caudally" ... *I'll flip a few pages ahead. I can't even read this book. It looks like English, but I can't understand. Hell, I can't even say any of the words except for superior and inferior—but superior and inferior to what?*

The formaldehyde smell was a bit overwhelming. "No," I said, "That's okay, you go ahead and cut John. I'm happy looking." *It has got to be close to time to leave. How come no one else looks anxious?*

Well, it *is* interesting that the muscles on the abdomen have a lengthwise structure that crisscrosses the abdomen almost like a girdle. Wow, look at that layer of yellow fat just beneath the skin. The muscle looks a bit like parboiled flank steak. Hmm, I didn't know human muscle looked so much like meat.

Okay, Mae, you can make yourself touch it. You have gloves on after all, unlike those professors dissecting bare-handed ... There, I touched it. Feels a bit like stringy meat. Oh, everyone's starting to leave. I knew time should be up. Out of the lab coat. Careful, don't let it touch any of my clothes. What's next?

We all went to lunch at a New York deli. *No worries*, I thought, *I'll wait 'til this evening to eat.* Sure, am glad I like vegetables.

Two weeks later, I was better. In gross anatomy lab, I could make incisions. By working through a medical vocabulary and terminology workbook I bought, I had come to understand the Latin roots of many medical words and how they described varying characteristics and locations. "Oblique" mean at an angle. If something was "anterior," it was toward the front of the person; "posterior," toward the person's back; "cephalic" meant having to do with the head. Directions were always given based on the patient's right and left. Cool. Things got better. I had all my books, and I could even manage to eat lunch after Gross Anatomy lab. But I still hadn't awakened and smelled the formaldehyde on the wind.

My cadaver partners and many of the other formerly *real* pre-meds had this terribly annoying habit of quizzing each other or showing off by recounting the most minute details and obscure names of minor blood vessels and nerves, and where they started and ended. They worried about the names of normal and rare variations of anatomy. I wondered, "What's the big deal? We can always look that up in a book." I was attempting to understand how the mechanical structure supports physiological and life activities. That other stuff was memorization. I figured the formerly *real* pre-meds were just being obsessive-compulsive again like in college. Yet, their behavior was so consistent; even Joan and Blaine did this. They would even go to the gross anatomy lab late at night to go over the dissection and the prosections of certain cadavers the professors had made to illustrate specific anatomical points.

One day, wanting to assure myself that indeed I, the engineer, was right and the pre-meds were wrong, I spoke to Professor Girkis. As he was demonstrating and naming what seemed to be a particularly obscure normal variation of the mesenteric arteries, I asked, "We're not really expected to know this are we?" Dr. Girkis, who very much resembled the fat man from the movie *Casablanca*, stopped and stared at me. I could see that any number of thoughts were clashing in his mind. Finally, he just simply answered, "*Yes.*" I can only imagine his incredulity.

Oops! I had ignored all the warning signs and explicit directions from the *real* pre-meds. My next weekend was determined in that moment. Early Saturday morning, I sat down with my human body atlases, dissection manual, gross anatomy textbooks, and several pads of paper, and began to memorize all the names, points of intersection, bifurcations, origins, and normal variants from the three weeks before when I had previously endeavored to "understand." I now understood that a different approach was needed. I read the text and dissections before class and reread materials after class. I even joined Joan and Blaine in a few midnight forays to the Gross Anatomy lab to review the materials in-the-flesh, so to speak.

I called my sister, Ada Sue, who was already in her fourth year of medical school, and I asked her advice. She sent me all her neuroanatomy and extra gross anatomy books.

Joan had already recruited me into a biochemistry study group. She and I reviewed microanatomy (the geography and functioning of the body's cells) together. I was constantly amazed by Joan's organization. She had a place for everything. Joan rewrote her notes from class and then filed and classified them in subject-specific binders. In class, Joan carried different colored pens and markers that she used to emphasize the lecture information. We also took notes as a group. Every lecture was taped and each student in the class took turns using these tapes to prepare lecture notes. These notes were then distributed to the entire class. Tests were pass/fail with an occasional high pass given out. There wasn't a low pass.

At Stanford, I had studied in the afternoon. My entire four years there, I had only pulled a couple of almost all-nighters, and then it had only been to finish typing papers. Occasionally I had stayed up until 2 a.m. to complete problem sets. In medical school, that all changed. Though I didn't do all-nighters, I often stayed up until 2 a.m. studying, especially during finals and for midterms. I would go to sleep at midnight and wake up at 4:30 a.m. to continue studying. On exam days, I always went to sleep by 1 a.m., even if I woke at 5 a.m. the next morning to do some "top off" studying. I believed it was better to be well rested so that my mind would have the best chance of remembering something I knew.

Never before had my classwork been such an all-encompassing focus of my life. I remember meeting people and seeing body parts, imagining where the splenic flexure of their colon was located. I visualized if the person I was talking to was accidently impaled by a spear, with entry at the anterior right mid-line seventh intercostal space and exit at posterior left tenth intercostal space, what structures would be affected. I was studying all the time by posing questions like those asked in Gross Anatomy quizzes. "What structures, beside their entire lives?"

Still, I was in New York City. The reasons I had wanted to be in NYC in the first place did not escape me. I found the Alvin Ailey Dance Studio on 58th Street and First Avenue. I spent what non-tuition, non-room money I had on modern dance classes. Whenever I left my class, as I was preparing to leave the building, I always heard drums upstairs. One day I ventured to the second floor and became totally enthralled with a Katherine Dunham technique dance class. Led by Joan Peters, the workout was hellacious, the choreography tough and rigorous, and the drums hypnotizing, as well as the drummers. (Damn, they looked good!) Dunham's technique, I believe, may best be described as African dance performed with a ballet technique. Katherine Dunham was one of the most exciting and original masters of dance in America. An anthropologist and dancer, she not only studied, but also learned African dancing. She started the Katherine Dunham Troupe in the 1940s. I definitely knew about her, but I had never learned her technique. From then on, every Tuesday and Thursday when I had the money, I walked the ten blocks to class to be invigorated and gain mental and physical energy. Then I would walk back no matter how cold or wet it was.

For recreation, Joan and I occasionally joined pickup basketball games in the Olin Hall gym. The gym remarkably resembled a gladiator pit. It had tiled walls all around, with I am sure, concrete beneath the linoleum floor. The distance from the out-of-bounds line to the wall was not more than 3 feet on the sidelines and maybe 6 feet behind the baskets. The majority of the folks playing there were *real* pre-meds, with all the attendant baggage, some interns, and residents. Many were not particularly athletically talented. It was dangerous down there. Injuries were common. Anger flared. I heard all types of inventive curse words (learn something new every day). Joan also played pool well so I would tag along with her and learn.

My eating habits changed. When I had arrived in New York, I did not drink sodas, did not eat candy, and only ate sweets I cooked myself. I ate very few processed foods. By the time I graduated from medical school, I was routinely eating hot dogs with mystery onions off the street vendor carts, Suzy Q's to stay awake when studying, and whatever I could scrounge up late at night from the nurses when on call at the hospital.

I went to Gil Scott-Heron concerts, Alvin Ailey and Dance Theater of Harlem performances, the New York City Ballet, and plays. Most Sundays I would wake up by 7 a.m., go to the deli, where I would get a cup of coffee and the *New York Times*. I'd enjoy the coffee and the *Times* before breaking out the books to study.

Later in the year, Joan let me in on a secret. She was surprised I was so involved in student politics, was so knowledgeable about African American history, and seemed a bit radical. She told me she figured when she saw I was from Stanford University I would be like, you know, a "California Girl." I would show up with a smiling surfer boy on my arm. Instead she and I wrote a script for the class Christmas show.

The skit was based on one of our very serious, astute, and quiet Introduction to Clinical Medicine professors becoming lost "Uptown" (read Harlem) on a Saturday night. We recruited Blaine to be a co-hoodlum with Joan. A classmate Joel was the hapless professor, and I played the "Woman on the Corner" to help him spice up his life. I still do not believe I had the nerve to wear that halter, those hot pants, *and* high-heel boots!

Extracurricular activities were an important part of school for me. My first year I helped put together a pamphlet for high school students to prevent prescription drug abuse with Rupa Redding, a second-year medical student. We even went into one of the schools to teach students about this. After spending a summer as a lab research assistant and traveling to Cuba with a medical student study group, I felt comfortable enough to become more active in student politics. As president of the Cornell chapter of the Student National Medical Association my second year, I helped coordinate a regional New York and New Jersey health and law fair with students from Columbia

University's law school and medical students from New Jersey Medical and Dental, Einstein, New York University, Cornell, and Columbia. During my third year, I was elected president of the Cornell Student Executive Committee, and during my last year I was the student representative for Cornell to the Association of American Medical Colleges. This fulfilled my need for social activism, but it also required a tremendous amount of energy. I committed political faux pas that caused me some grief with the administration, but I also learned about the workings of medical schools and the politics of medicine.

I CAN LEARN NEW TRICKS

By my second year, I had adjusted to the rhythm of medical school. The first class on the schedule was Microbiology and Microbiology Lab. This time I was ready. I knew how to pay attention to detail. I already had all my books. Y'all, I was ready. However, I was just not prepared for the fact that the blood for the experiment to understand how antibodies are produced as a result of typhoid vaccination would come from the students—us. They got me again!

After the lecture, we went into the lab, took seats and were told that the person next to us would be our lab partner. Cool. Then we had to take blood from one another, before giving each other injections of typhoid vaccine.

Not so cool. Not only did I intensely dislike needles, but the guy sitting next to me, my new lab partner, looked like he couldn't tie his shoes on the first try. (No offense meant, but you notice these things when someone is about to impale you with a two-inch needle.) This was the first time the vast majority of us had ever tried to take blood, so the microbiology department generously supplied written instructions. Great! But let's just say my buddy was not successful on the first try. I have small veins. Experienced lab techs occasionally have problems with getting blood from me. After several sticks, our professor eventually had to draw my blood. (Yes, I was able to get blood from my partner the first time.) Next came the vaccinations. My partner did a great job. Overall, on a Friday afternoon, the lab was not too bad, until that evening when I felt hot, feverish, headachy, nauseated, and fatigued, and my shoulder started to throb. These were the "minor" side effects of the vaccination our professor had said would last only twenty-four hours. Oh yeah, the arm soreness could last up to three days.

The highlight of second year was taking Physical Diagnosis and getting our medical instruments. Owning a stethoscope meant you really were becoming a doctor. Actually, you had to order your stuff before Physical Diagnosis class started.

That doctor stuff is expensive. My budget was limited, so I couldn't get the classic doctor bag. I didn't like it anyway. I got a stethoscope, sphygmomanometer (blood pressure cuff), an ophthalmoscope/otoscope combination, a reflex hammer, tuning forks (what are they for?), a flashlight, and a white jacket. Now we're talking. We learned on one another how to listen to the heart, examine the eyes, assess the integrity of the spinal efferent and afferent peripheral nerves (nerves to and from the spinal cord) using the reflex hammer and tuning forks (so that's what they're for), how to estimate the size of the liver, and use new words like "boborygmy" for stomach growling.

I could do this; in fact, I was pretty good with physical exams on my classmates. I soon learned it was quite different asking a stranger to take off their clothes so I could examine them naked. Even though I helped patients maintain their dignity with strategically placed small sheets, what about my embarrassment?

One of the greatest side-benefits for me of the third-year clinical rotations in medical training was realizing that one can stay up for thirty-six hours and still function mentally and physically. One learns not to resent circumstances because things happen to go awry or resent people because they get sick at times inconvenient to your schedule. Seemingly fighting it every step of the way, I learned to be precise and thorough so that my patients did not pay for my sloppiness with their lives or have sequela (bad outcomes), which I could have prevented with a bit more diligence.

A SOUTHERLY WIND BLOWS...
Africa

I spent the summer between my second year and third year of medical school in Kenya, a country in East Africa. Arriving there was really like reaching a destination I had dreamed about and moved toward all my life. From childhood I wore my hair short because of Miriam Makeba, I danced to Olatunji, I took African dance lessons in college, and I majored in African studies. Later, I would work for the Peace Corps in West Africa.

What do I remember most about my first trip to Africa? Several things. The trip started off with a cacophony of altered plans salvaged because fortunately, I had done a lot of preparation. I had studied every student travel book and information guide on East Africa that I could find, including all the various air routes between Nairobi and the United States.

When I arrived the Kennedy Airport to travel to London, I found the flight had been canceled due to mechanical problems and that to get on the new plane I would have to pay more for my seat. The replacement flight was delayed getting into London, and I missed my connecting flight. The airline counter agent had sympathy and gave me the last first-class seat on a flight to Copenhagen that would connect with a Scandinavian Airlines flight to Nairobi without charge. (It was my first time in Europe. There may have been a teardrop involved; I'm not sure). I made the connection in Copenhagen. As that flight was in the air, a light mist filled part of the cabin and, because that particular type of aircraft had had some prior safety problems, the crew decided to land in Zürich and have the plane checked. So all the passengers had to deplane and spend the night in Zürich. We had half a day and I got to take a bus tour of the city. Then we reboarded back on the plane, and I was finally on my way to Nairobi, for real.

Seeing the shore of North Africa as the plane crossed the Mediterranean was magical. The sea sparkled blue and green. Then beneath us appeared the golden-brown sands of the Sahara Desert. The Sahara Desert! Where camel caravans had linked West African empires with Egypt. The Sahara Desert! Where many believe that thousands of years ago, societies flourished in a savannah, before drought and time gradually turned it into an ocean of desolation. The Sahara! Home of the fabled city of knowledge, Timbuktu. Y'all, this was the desert with the pyramids and was where the pharaohs had lived! A vastness that could hold the entire continental United States. I was over Africa! Africa existed. It was real and some of my ancestors had come from this place.

My travel was supported through a study grant I had proposed to the International Travelers Association and student loan money I had borrowed to cover my expenses while I was in Kenya. I took on several jobs there. I worked with the the African Medical Education and Research Foundation (AM-REF), formerly known as the Flying Doctors. The Flying Doctors began as a group of physicians and other healthcare professionals who would travel to remote areas of Kenya and East Africa to provide health services, particularly surgery, to people who might otherwise go without. The Flying Doctors used airplanes because roads were often unpassable or nonexistent. Later they expanded their work to include more epidemiology, the study of people and the illnesses they have, and how those illnesses originate.

With AMREF, I helped perform a community health survey and diagnosis in the Embu district near Mt. Kenya. The team I accompanied walked from homestead to homestead in rural villages assessing the health of the people; measured the height and weight of children; counted the number of people per household, and logged their vaccination status. I also assisted with the surgery performed using drip-ether anesthesia. I worked for a week in a hospital and clinic in Voi district assisting a British surgeon. After touristing in Mombasa for four days I arrived in the evening on local transport wearing a kitenge cloth wrapped around my waist and a tee shirt. The head nurse mistook me for a member of his ethnic group, the Taita, rudely speaking Swahili to him, instead of "our" Taita mother tongue. I was really fitting in! In Voi, I saw a baby delivered for the first time. Amazing. It looked like it *hurt*! Once a herd of zebras crossed the road in front of us illuminated only by the car's headlights as we traveled at night and in a remote section of the Voi National Park.

When in Nairobi, the capital city of Kenya, I roomed with Laura Tuthill, a fellow New York City graduate student whom I had met at the Jomo Kenyatta Airport arrivals as we went through immigration control at eleven o'clock at night.

Neither of us had a confirmed place to stay that night because of the plane mishaps, so we partnered on the spot and at 1 a.m. found a cheap, tacky hotel to stay in, which sufficed until we found permanent quarters. Laura was there for a summer internship with the United Nations environmental program office. We stayed with a Kenyan dentist who had been a student at the University of Maryland, where Laura's father was a professor who had hosted the dentist when he was a student in the U.S. The dentist was returning the favor by hosting Laura. I stayed with the dentist, his family, and Laura when I was not traveling outside of Nairobi with AMREF.

Through the dentist, I was introduced to private clinical health care in Kenya. I also met members of the Kenyan Hindi community. Though the dentist was Luo, one of the major Kenyan ethnic groups, and of African ancestry, many of the other dentists were from India. I helped the dentists' organization by editing transcripts of guest lectures of the Kenya Dental Association meetings.

Nairobi 1979 was an attractive city with bougainvillea vines — magenta, fuschia, pink, white, orange, and red— spilling over the walls and center dividers of main thoroughfares. Large market places sprawled. Odors of piquant spices, fish, meat, and fruits in all states of freshness wafted in the air. Open stalls were hung with brightly colored fabric and baskets for sale. The stores displayed household products and second-hand electronics. When it rained, puddles formed in the mud. Extreme poverty was apparent, right next door to extravagant wealth. Old colonial-style houses were scattered in high-income neighborhoods. Downtown was filled with shops, restaurants, and office buildings. Mostly two- or three-story rectangular, stucco buildings with flat roofs lined the streets. Occasionally, there were high-rise buildings up to 20 stories tall like the circular building destroyed when the U.S. embassy was bombed in 1998, that bespoke modernization. There were large modern conference centers and movie theatres. I saw *Moonraker* in one. James Bond was a hit in Kenya.

I rode the crowded city buses around Nairobi and learned to muscle my way inside. (Not too much trouble for a former Chicagoan and current New Yorker used to riding the "El" train and the subways.) Matatus, however, were a different story. These privately-owned vans and small buses regularly picked up people and carried them to their destinations. The doors hung off. The crowds inside put Tokyo subway cars to shame. New York cabbies would not stand a chance driving against them. My heart was not up to the challenge. I avoided them.

In Nairobi, it was great to be able to go into any hair salon and get my hair done. My hair was the norm. And no one was trying toget me to straighten or relax it. They did cornrows routinely. One day, a shop, and its people stand out in my mind. When the proprietress asked the woman cornrowing my hair how much I owed, the hairdresser did her calculations out loud in Swahili. She did not know I could understand. She said she would have to charge me a bit more because I had a "kichwa kubwa" and "nyele nyinigi"—a big head and a lot of hair. When I laughed, everyone in the shop looked around and laughed, too. It was the camaraderie and belonging that felt so wonderful.

I was ready to be in Africa. I was well-prepared. I knew Swahili. I had studied the politics of the religion. I had studied the history and culture before, throughout, and after colonialism. I knew the geography and some of the issues of development. I had completed a four-week course in parasitology with an emphasis on diseases of the tropics just prior to coming. But I really wasn't exactly ready for Kawangware, where I helped with some community medicine projects while in Nairobi. Kawangware was unexpected.

Kawangware, a huge slum, sat on a crowded expanse of land on the outskirts of Nairobi. People who left the rural villages for the perceived advantages of the capital city gathered there. Many of them could not afford Nairobi and Nairobi did not welcome them. So people ended up on this bare expanse of red dirt, where ditches along the side of the road served as open sewers. The ditches overflowed with too much rain. Poorly constructed mud homes with zinc-pan roofs over-heated and leaked. Lean-to structures built of discarded, but recycled pieces of lumber kept the rain out, sometimes, and the goats and chickens in or out, depending on the resident's preference. All around, I could see the despair in people's faces, but I could feel the hope and determination in their hearts as they swept porches and carried water on their heads. Illness lurked around corners in darkened lean-to shacks, but the possibilities for tomorrow swirled the red dirt in the streets, as children pushed each other in small carts. I was at Kawagare with AMREF to develop training materials, for public health workers and volunteers about clean water and first aid.

I remember the conversations and arguments I had with Kenyans about African Americans. To make a long story short, one told me that Kenyans thought the Black folks in the Tarzan movies were African Americans playing African Americans. So, Tarzan movies managed to misrepresent Black folk on both sides of the Atlantic in one fell swoop.

I left Kenya after eight weeks to travel north to Egypt, Greece, and Israel. I would spend two weeks traveling before returning to the United States and the intense medical school third-year clinical rotations.

I stepped off the plane in Cairo, planning to stretch my funds by traveling around on my own. I had already contacted a student hostel, I had a guidebook, and I knew most of the places I wanted to go. Plans changed quickly. I decided to sign up for formal, organized escorted tours after being leered at by soldiers at the airport, even though I had worn a very modest, long skirt and a blouse with quarter-length sleeves. I looked around the airport and I realized most of the signs were in Arabic. Not only couldn't I read them I also couldn't even visually remember the letters. I realized Egypt would be difficult to travel around safely and cheaply on my own, so I traveled with a young New Zealand couple I met at a travel service when signing on for a tour package at the Cairo airport.

I visited the pyramids of Giza and the bazaars of Cairo. I saw, as well, the layers of religion and evidence of competing forces that this pivotal locale of human civilization had experienced. The early history of Christianity in Cairo represented by the Coptic Church was fascinating. Islamic history came afterwards. At the Luxor Temple, on the Nile, the immense scale to which everything was built during the time of the pharaohs took my breath away as did the vibrancy of the colors of the hieroglyphics after all the thousands of years. The tombs in the Valley of Kings and Queens were cool providing relief from the noon sun that burned my skin in thirty minutes. I even got to go into Tutankhamun's—King Tut's—tomb.

My return airplane ticket had me travel through the Athens airport, but I was forced to skip seeing Greece. I had spent all my money, except for about seventy dollars to book the formal tours in Egypt. So I boarded the plane for Israel, hoping to charge a tour package on the credit card my mother had given me for emergencies. On the Olympic Airways flight, I sat next to an American Jewish woman who was returning to her home in Quiryat Tivon after vacationing in the United States for a few weeks. We struck up a conversation, and, incredibly, she invited me to stay with her and travel around Israel the next week as she had some time off.

I stayed with her in a kibbutz, met a former operative of Mossad, the Israeli Secret Service, visited the Sea of Galilee, and the hillside where Jesus Christ is said to have given the Sermon on the Mount. One day, we sat talking in 100-degree weather after my companions had convinced me to get into a hot sulfur spring to cool off on a hillside overlooking a flat expanse of land. The former Mossad operative pointed out that I was looking at the Golan Heights and Syria, just 10 kilometers away. He explained that Israel was a thin strip of land that was difficult to protect and told me his recollection of the Seven Day War.

In Jerusalem, I went to the Dome of the Rock, which I learned was the holiest place in Islam after Mecca. It was said to be the site from which Muhammad ascended to heaven. That very same place is said to be where Abraham was to have sacrificed his son.

My host dropped me off near the Wailing Wall, where she would meet me later. She did not feel comfortable in the Arab Quarters of Old Jerusalem. I followed the Via Dolorosa, the path Christ was supposed to have taken as he carried the cross on the way to his crucifixion. One of the stops on the walk was at an old church that had an area open below its cellar. Cobblestone streets from the days of Christ were visible and cisterns built by the Romans still stored rain water. The journey ended at the Church of the Holy Sepulchre, which some say is the site of Christ's tomb.

From all these places in Egypt and Israel, all the people, the ideas, one on top of the other, Judaism, Christianity, Islam, Palestine, Israel, Romans, Nubians, and pharaohs, I began to understand the complexity of politics—and I also saw faith. I felt the wind gathering energy, and I understood that until we humans fully acknowledge how intertwined we are with one another, there will be endless suffering. Until people are willing to recognize and honestly, openly, and transparently discuss inequities, wrongs, aggression, violence, peace offerings, and history, not only will individuals suffer, but so will the planet.

VORTEX

When you graduate from medical school you just have a medical degree. You do not have a license to practice medicine. To get a license, in most states, you must complete at least an internship; then you can work and also pay back all the loans you accumulated while in college and medical school. After internships, physicians complete residency programs to specialize in things like pediatrics and psychiatry. During the time of my internship, new doctors, interns. and residents, were paid very modestly to work in hospitals about eighty to ninety hours per week. While doing this, new physicians gain experience in patient care under the supervision of more experienced doctors. It's not involuntary servitude, but it could feel like it sometimes.

I went to medical school because I wanted to do biomedical engineering research, I never intended to practice medicine. So I had never intended to pursue a residency program. While at Cornell, my travels to Cuba, Kenya, and a Cambodian refugee camp in Thailand taught me that I was fascinated by medicine in developing countries—primary care and basic medicine. I had learned so much about the world and myself. I knew that I wanted to have a longer experience in those environments.

Therefore, I decided to apply for what was called a one-year rotating internship with nothing—graduate school or medical residency—scheduled afterward. Having nothing scheduled would force me to plan for something overseas. I would come back and apply to graduate school in engineering later.

Back up, rethink this. At least that's what the deans at Cornell said. I was summoned by two of them. They implored me to apply for a full residency program. After all, they told me, I was graduating from one of the best medical schools in the country. Cornell alumni were expected not only to be board certified in surgery, pediatrics, obstetrics and gynecology, internal medicine and other specialties, but also to do more in-depth fellowships afterward. You know, like pulmonology or neonatology care. Here I was just doing an internship, and a flexible internship at that.

I explained my plan to go to work in the developing world, then go onto graduate school in engineering, to pursue bio-medical engineering research. One dean said I was making a terrible mistake. He explained that in ten years I would be far behind my fellow classmates and feel less accomplished than them.

I did feel wary, but I decided this time not to get the classical degree and go to the regular route as I had at Stanford. Just like Joan frequently joked, it seemed I was wasting a perfectly good clinical medicine slot and doing something somewhat strange and "California" with it.

I spent the following year in Los Angeles at the Los Angeles County/University of Southern California Medical Center—(LAC/USC Med Center), the largest Los Angeles County hospital, gaining more experience in pediatrics, infectious diseases, surgery, oncology (cancer medicine), obstetrics and gynecology, and emergency medicine. That year served to solidify my practical knowledge in general practice medicine. At LA County Med Center, one certainly got to work with many different illnesses and types of patients. During that year I also made it my business to investigate opportunities to travel overseas and to work in a developing country.

I researched and applied to many organizations and noted on my applications that I could work as a physician or an engineer, whichever was needed. After speaking with a Peace Corps recruiter about a position in Papua, New Guinea, setting up a computerized database on the nutritional status of the islanders, I was informed of an opening not for a volunteer, but a paid staff job with responsibilities for the health of volunteers. I applied for and was selected for this position in West Africa.

As the Area Peace Corps Medical Officer for Sierra Leone and Liberia, at twenty-six years old, I was responsible for the health of all the U.S. Peace Corps volunteers, staff members, and embassy personnel of Sierra Leone and the Peace Corps volunteers in Liberia. I managed a medical office, a laboratory, a pharmacy, and volunteer health training as well as acted as the primary care doctor. I encountered diseases I had only read about in tropical medicine textbooks. I worked with Sierra Leonean physicians and nurses trained in the best schools in England and Germany, but who were at times forced to work with little or no equipment, medication, or supplies. I cared for a patient in Freetown with acute encephalitis when there was no electricity. I assisted in the appendectomy of my best friend's son; I oversaw the autopsy of a person who may have died of Lassa Fever, a hemorrhagic virus and the one infectious disease that had truly frightened me when I had read about it in medical school.

On call twenty-four hours a day, seven days a week for two-and-a-half years, in a place that could be so unforgiving of mistakes, I gained flexibility, knowledge, interpersonal relationship skills, and an appreciation of the challenges life poses to so many people on this planet.

The Harmattan, the winds blowing off the Sahara Desert in December, blew cool, dry air and brought haze to the skies of West Africa, while its dust carried nutrients all the way to the Amazon. In spring, the Hamattan abated, the sky cleared, and light rains fell. In a similar manner, the dilemma I faced—how to balance and integrate my love of advanced science and technologies with my love for travel, other countries, and other cultures was solved. The insights I gained into the misconceptions of lifestyles and the challenges and opportunities in poor countries nourished my imagination. I understood. What we decide to do with our talents is up to each one of us and is based on our view of life and our desires. My talents in the physical sciences and social sciences were as applicable and important for the development of inexpensive but effective systems to bring clean drinking water to millions of people in rural villages as they were to helping a person suffering from renal disease in the most prestigious hospital in New York City.

WIND CURRENTS
Reality Leads Fantasy

"*The phase distortion is clearing. Transport window will open in two minutes,*" Lieutenant Palmer reported. She watched Commander Riker, Lieutenant Commander La Forge, and Lieutenant Worf as they waited for Lieutenant Riker to report to the transporter room, Lieutenant Palmer, a tall female human from Earth with a very close-cropped hairstyle was not normally on transporter room duty. In fact, she was new to the crew of the Starship *Enterprise*. Her last mission had been on the Space Shuttle *Endeavour* over 200 years before. Wait a minute … in addition to the transporter problem that created two Rikers, there's a little time distortion issue here.

My appearance on the *Star Trek: The Next Generation* episode "Second Chances" in 1993 was the completion of a circle that had begun in 1966 the first time I saw *Star Trek* on television. At LeVar Burton's invitation, I became the first and only USS *Enterprise* crew member to have actually gone into space at that time. I felt quite honored to be on the set, and, in a way, to become a small part of the *Star Trek* family.

When the *Star Trek* series premiered on network television, I was only nine years old, but I already knew that I would travel in space. I had a set of encyclopedias that gave the step-by-step details of how humans would arrive on the surface of the moon. I had latched onto the study of how the universe began, how stars were formed, and how life began and evolved on Earth and colonization of other planets as lifelong interests.

Much to adults' dismay, I had defiantly pronounced that NASA and anyone else who tried to explain as reasonable the idea that women were not suited to be astronauts were nonsensical. There was no explanation except that the folks controlling the programs stupidly just did not want women to participate. I stand by that to this day.

As I said, I had already decided that I would go into space. The fact that all the U.S. astronauts then were white men just made it a little more difficult, a challenge.

Though the Russians had sent up a woman cosmonaut, Valentina Tereshkova in 1964, not many people around me seemed to share my conviction that I would travel to space, which made things a bit complicated. My parents supported all my science projects and whims, but I still don't know if they were true believers or shared my enthusiasm for space-flight.

Then came *Star Trek*, with Lieutenant Uhura, Mr. Spock, and Lieutenant Sulu. Wow! Somewhere, someone else believed that other kinds of people would populate spaceships from Earth. Humans of all genders and ethnicities would be in space. Here was affirmation. *Star Trek* immediately captured my imagination and respect. Amid the scares of nuclear proliferation and annihilation, moral and ethical conflicts concerning criminal justice, nationalism in colonies, the second and third waves of racial riots in the United States, and the promise and uncertainty of physical science advances, *Star Trek* presented a hopeful view of humanity and the future.

Star Trek dealt with issues of our time, social as well as technological, in the safety and glaring spotlight of the future and science fiction. The show tackled topics like the bitter animosity between two creatures based on what they considered to be incredible differences: the characters were literally half black and half white on different sides of their bodies. In the episode, these differences in their society heralded bigotry and sparked oppression. *Star Trek* episodes considered whether violence is ever acceptable. What is the difference between good and evil when both seek conquest of the other? Why shouldn't humans be used for experiments and gambling as we use other animals today? There was quasi-scientific talk and mysteries in the middle of societal issues. How do we define life? Must intelligent life look like us? Must it be based on carbon? Can computers supplant humans in command structures and decision making? Just what is "warp factor one" and how does anti-matter drive an engine?

Amidst all these positive affirmations, incongruous human foibles still flourished. Every time Bones, the physician, wanted to insult Mr. Spock, he would say something disparaging about Spock's Vulcan blood or mixed human and Vulcan parentage. Ditto if Captain Kirk wanted to insult Spock. An episode that absolutely outraged me was when it was revealed that women could not be starship captains. (This was in 1966-68, pre-Captain Janeway on *Star Trek: Voyager* and Captain Georgiou on *Star Trek: Discovery*). The woman, who was more qualified than Kirk, switched places with him through an ingenious mind-body switching device just so that she could have the command of a starship. She then became overbearing and made poor, emotional decisions. And Kirk, inside the woman's body, was the calm, reasonable person he never was in masculine garb. You know, I just had a problem with that whole scenario.

My overall favorite characters were Mr. Spock and Lt. Uhura. Mr. Spock was "The Man." I thought he was particularly cool, not only because he was brilliant, but also because of his insight into humans and their behavior. He provided that reflecting board to make sure we paid attention. His "lack of emotions" and logic were an interesting approach to dealing with life.

Lt. Uhura. What can I say? I always wanted to see her on screen. I believe she was the first woman to appear regularly on television in a technical role. She was intelligent, skillful, gorgeous, cool, and looked a bit like me and the women around me. She had a wonderful soothing voice and manner. I was disappointed that she did not get more airtime.

I met Nichelle Nichols, the actress who played Lt. Uhura, after I was an astronaut. In fact, I was at Kennedy Space Center (KSC) participating in the Terminal Countdown Demonstration Test (TCDT) for STS-26, the first launch after the *Challenger* accident when I heard her on the radio. Ms. Nichols was being interviewed on a morning talk show to publicize a *Star Trek* convention taking place in Orlando, Florida, over Labor Day weekend. Now, not being a "real" Trekkie—you know those people who wear *Star Trek* costumes, buy the paraphernalia and schematics of the starships, and know all the titles of the episodes — I had never been to a convention. But I thought it would be cool to meet Lt. Uhura, because in some ways, she was instrumental to my being at KSC.

Nichelle Nichols and her company, Women in Motion, were pivotal in the recruitment of the first women and minority astronauts in 1976-77. When NASA decided to admit women to the astronaut program and actively sought non-white male participation, they ran into a problem. Over the years of being rejected and seeing only one face of "the right stuff," many other faces having "the right stuff"—women and men of color—didn't believe NASA was serious. So for the class of astronauts that would crew the new reusable vehicle, the space shuttle, NASA received very few applications from those previously spurned groups. NASA looked for a way to convince folks they were serious. NASA and Nichelle found each other. Nichelle, with no personal compensation, underwent aspects of astronauts' training, made public service announcements, and traveled across the country to draw the attention of individuals with qualifications to become astronauts, but who did not respond to NASA alone. I personally remember the public service announcements and the effort. But alas, I was still in college then, and through precocious, too young and without a college degree. NASA would have to wait.

Back to 1988. I recruited the Kennedy Space Center Life Sciences physician, Dr. Irene Long, who was also a big science fiction and Star Trek fan, to go with me. Here's the scene. We arrived at the convention in Orlando. I was a little bit shy, but I thought what the heck, I'll just go up to the convention producers and tell them who I am and that I want to meet Ms. Nichols. Right? Exactly who was I? I was dressed casually in white khaki pants and a striped blouse and looked younger than my thirty-one years. I was an African American woman at a Trekkie convention trying to see one of the legends of *Star Trek*. Would they believe I was an astronaut as I smiled and said so? Well, it was worth the try.

Surprise, surprise. After I found the fellow in charge, I announced, "My name is Dr. Mae Jemison. I am an astronaut working at Kennedy Space Center, and I am here to meet Ms. Nichelle Nichols. I think she might also want to meet me." Guess what? He told me to follow him and he would ask her.

We walked to her hotel room. He told us to wait outside the door. I didn't know if Nichelle even knew my name. Next thing I knew, I heard her saying, "You have Mae Jemison waiting outside? Bring her in immediately." I was embraced in a warm hug. And we have been close friends ever since.

Due to her mother's illness Nichelle was unable to come to the launch of my spaceflight, but I spoke with her the night before. And I began my shifts on orbit with a variation of Lt. Uhura's trademark calls: "*Huntsville,* Endeavour. *All hailing frequencies are open.*" The circle was complete.

HARNESSING EXPLOSIONS

ENDEAVOUR

"**M**ae, come up to the flight deck," I heard over my headset as I worked to complete the stowage of the orange launch and entry suits. Still in my lightweight thermal underwear from launch, I pushed off and floated through the opening from the mid-deck to the flight deck. Hoot, the commander of STS-47 Spacelab J, the fiftieth flight of the space shuttle, pointed out the window. "*Chicago is coming up.*"

I peered out.

The first thing I saw from space was my hometown. Chicago looked just like it did on the map I learned in school. The grayish color of the concrete, barren land, and buildings of the metropolitan areas outlined the city against the green of the surrounding farmland. I thought about being a little girl down there and smiled. I watched Chicago leisurely pass from sight. My hometown passed from horizon to horizon in less than five minutes.

I thanked Hoot for calling me and returned to the mid-deck to complete the stowage timeline. I removed the launch chairs, finished the suit storage, pulled down some cue cards, and put up others. Now alone, 163 nautical miles above Earth's surface, we, the seven-member crew of the orbiter *Endeavour*, on its second flight, were transforming it from a rocket into a space laboratory.

During the mission, I was scheduled on the "Blue" shift with Drs. Jan Davis and Jay Apt. The Blue shift worked during the hours that mainly corresponded to night time in the United States; the "Red" shift corresponded to daytime. Jay, who had his Ph.D. in physics from Harvard, was on his second mission, and was the MS-2 (Mission Specialist 2). His job was to attend to those things that kept the shuttle *Endeavour* itself operating smoothly during our shift. Jan, who had a Ph.D. in mechanical engineering from the University of Huntsville, entered the astronaut program with me in August 1987 and was part of the payload crew. She was married to another member of our crew, Air Force Colonel Mark Lee. Jan, Mark, and I had trained for over two years, much of that time in Japan, to learn about the experiments we'd be conducting on this flight. Japan is where we met and trained with Dr. Mohri Mamoru, a Ph.D. in fluid physics, who rounded out the payload crew. Mamoru was a Payload Specialist on his first spaceflight, and was the first Japanese national to fly aboard the space shuttle.

Mark and Mamoru were on the Red shift along with our commander, Navy Captain Robert "Hoot" Gibson, and the pilot, Air Force Captain Curt Brown. Hoot and Curt worked like Jay to keep the shuttle running smoothly during the Red shift.

The job of the payload crew—Jan, Mamoru, Mark, and I— was to do all the "real work." The experiments that the shuttle carried into orbit took advantage of the microgravity environment. This is an environment where objects have very little weight. Gravity is still present, but its effects are counteracted by the "free fall" of our orbit. We worked in the "shirt-sleeve" conditions of the Spacelab, a 23-foot-long pressurized structure built by the European Space Agency (ESA) that fit in the payload bay of the shuttle. The Spacelab was a reusable laboratory that could be installed in any of the various space shuttle orbiters: the *Discovery*, the *Atlantis*, the *Columbia*, or the *Endeavour*. (By the way, the airplane-looking part is called the "orbiter" because it is the only piece of the launch stack that actually orbits Earth.) Our mission, called Spacelab J, carried over forty-four different experiments, ranging from material sciences and development of new semiconductor materials (that's the stuff computer chips are made of) to biology and how frog embryos develop in weightlessness. The experiments were designed by investigators from across Japan and the United States. Some of the investigators or scientists worked for NASA or NASDA (what the Japanese Space Agency was called at that time). Others were researchers from universities and private industry.

We had seven scheduled days of experiments. Additional days could be added if the shuttle supplies lasted. Our orbital inclination was such that we crossed the equator at a 57° angle and so were able to see northern Japan—in fact we could see all of the earth between the latitudes 57° north and 57° south of the equator. On lift-off, the shuttle's main engines combined with the primary lifting capabilities of the solid rocket boosters generated 7,781,400 pounds of thrust accelerating the *Endeavour* from zero miles per hour to over 17,000 miles per hour. In the roughly eight minutes it took us to ascend to space, we not only reached 17,500 miles per hour, but also traveled over the Atlantic where the solid rocket boosters dropped into the ocean to be retrieved for reuse. As we climbed to an altitude of over 160 nautical miles, we flew over Africa to the Indian Ocean, where we attained orbit, the main engines shut down, and the external tank, separated from the orbiter. The external tank, which had supplied all the fuel for the shuttle's main engine on ascent, tumbled into the atmosphere and burned up. Meanwhile, the orbiter and its crew began the process of establishing our home in space.

Once we were in space, Hoot fired the Orbital Maneuvering System (OMS) engines, to "circularize" our orbit from an elliptical shape so that our lowest point (perigee) and highest point (apogee) were basically the same altitude. Hoot, Curt, and Jay opened the payload bay doors and used the Reaction Control System (RCS) jets, to change Endeavour's attitude so that its tail pointed toward the the Earth. This positioning of the shuttle to Earth's surface gave us the best radio communication signals with the ground and allowed us to radiate all the heat that the on board equipment would generate to the coldness of space. The orbiter's radiators, or cooling system, are part of the payload bay doors.

Meanwhile Jan, Mark, Mamoru, and I worked to prepare the rest of the shuttle for our week of experiments. It all seemed so simple. The panels filled with switches and circuit breakers were so easily understood now. All the procedures flowed smoothly. All so easy and uncomplicated from what I would have imagined when I first stepped inside of a shuttle mock-up in August 1987 after reporting to the Johnson Space Center in Houston, Texas as an astronaut candidate, or AS-CAN as they called us.

THIS IS HOUSTON ...

On a cold, rainy January evening in 1987, I grabbed my mail as I ran up the stairs to the second-floor landing of my apartment building in West Los Angeles. I was a little tired after working all day as a doctor at Cigna Health Plans the West L.A. facility on Sepulveda Boulevard. I had just taken an aerobics class at Voight Fitness in West Hollywood after work, so I was in sweaty tights, leotards, Reeboks, and a sweatshirt. Now I was home and could shower, eat, and rest.

My cat Sneeze, whom I got as a tiny kitten in Sierra Leone, jumped up and greeted me at the door with lots of love and affection. His green eyes and loving caresses on my leg alerted me. I wondered what he had been up to and looked around my one-bedroom apartment for tattletale signs of misbehavior. Nothing wrong that I could find easily, so I plopped on the couch. Sneeze climbed on my lap and meowed loudly to give me a proper welcome home.

I shuffled through the mail. There it was. I thought I had

seen it. An envelope from NASA. I opened it and found forms to be completed for background checks and security clearances for my application to the astronaut program. Wow! At least NASA was still interested. It had been a year since I had last seen this same set of forms. But before I had a chance to fill them out and return them, the Space Shuttle *Challenger* had blown up on January 28, 1986. And all the world had just stopped to stare in disbelief and try to understand.

NASA postponed the astronaut selection process for 1986 and informed the applicants that they would keep their applications on file. The selection office would let us know when NASA would start looking for new astronauts again.

The requests for updates had arrived in fall of 1986 and I had immediately completed and returned them. So on that January night in 1987, I completed the security clearance forms and sent them in quickly. I waited to see what would happen.

A few weeks later, I received a telephone call asking me if I was available to come to Johnson Space Center (JSC) in Houston, the following week for interviews. NASA interviewed a total of about 100 people out of approximately 2,000 qualified applicants. Fifteen of us would ultimately be selected.

In a week? Well, yeah sure. But, how was I going to get a week off from patient care on such short notice without everyone knowing? I didn't want folks to know I was applying to be an astronaut. I mean, who would think you were real or sane? So, I went to Beverly, the office manager, and told her not to tell anyone. I told one other person, my friend, the X-ray technician Sylvia Tanner. Well, the secret didn't last. Of course, when I got back from Houston everyone knew where I had been.

Believe it or not, I was almost more excited when called for the astronaut interview than when I was selected. Why? Because I had looked good on paper! My college and medical school transcripts that I had fretted over were fine. The recommendations, my job experience, even the two-and-a-half years I had spent in West Africa as a physician, which I thought would seem strange, must have been good. Wow, I would get to go to Johnson Space Center!

The next day I dashed to the UCLA bookstore at lunch time and bought books on the history of space exploration to study before I got to JSC. I called to arrange my flights to Houston. I tried to control my excitement. I only told my family. I got a couple of new suits to wear in Houston for the interviews. Darn, I had just cut my hair into this slightly hip-hop Afro style. Just a week prior, I had been wearing it parted down the middle and up in two "schoolmarm-ish" braids. Now how would I look conservative enough for the people at

JSC? *Well, I gotta go with what I've got now. I just won't spike and color the bangs blue,* I thought.

... IS THERE A PROBLEM?

So what do you do over a week of astronaut interviews? There were medical exams of every form. Through the exams, the flight surgeons were attempting to establish that the applicants were physiologically normal. After all, astronauts are placed in abnormal, hazardous environments, and it's most helpful to begin with as normal a physiology as possible. They looked for all types of chronic illness and physical and psychological anomalies. I had the passing thought that perhaps some of my patients got together and called up to give them suggestions for what tests to run so I'd know what it felt like. There were eye exams with dilated pupils by ophthalmologists, sigmoidoscopy, sinus x-rays, blood tests, muscle strength tests, hearing tests, psychological tests, and a full physical exam. A personal favorite of mine was an isolation/claustrophobia test where I was asked to sit inside a 3-foot diameter balloon with air blowing in it for 30 minutes. I was to write my impressions of the experience afterwards as well as write up any modifications I would make to the sphere as a space rescue and transfer device. I got in and started to hum and sing to myself and then fell asleep. The operator said I was the first one he had seen do that.

During my physical, the flight surgeon told me he heard a heart murmur. I told him I knew all about it and had first learned of it in medical school. The doctors at Cornell said it was a functional flow murmur, a fancy medical way of saying that because of the shape of my chest wall and the way my heart was positioned, one could hear the blood flowing through it. None of my medical school professors had ever been concerned about it, but the flight surgeons were.

After the physical, I just sat and smiled to myself, thinking it was a good try. I was sad that a non-life-threatening murmur was going to disqualify me as an astronaut, but that was life. The flight surgeon said he would refer me to a cardiologist for an echocardiogram to see if there was any abnormality with my heart valves. Great! I wasn't out of yet. Once the echocardiogram was done and read, I was examined. The cardiologist agreed—it was just a "flow murmur."

I left Houston still in the game. Weeks went by. Some of my friends called me to tell me that they had been interviewed by the FBI. One joked, "I told them, 'Yes she can take and follow orders, but she is not going to walk off a cliff without a damned good explanation.'" I spoke with the FBI and told them all my secrets. I waited. It was almost like the trip to

Houston had never happened. Things settled down. I continued to attend business and engineering classes at UCLA at night and worked at Cigna as a general practicioner in the day. By this time, I had been transferred to the main Cigna facility closer to downtown Los Angeles.

One afternoon in June, I was seeing a patient for lower back pain. As was my custom, I spoke to him about his symptoms and stepped out of the room to record some notes in the chart and wait for him to undress. As soon as I walked into my office, my desk phone rang. I picked it up.

"Dr. Jemison, may I help you?"

"Is this Dr. Mae Jemison?"

"Yes, it is."

"This is George Abbey at NASA, and we wanted to know if you still wanted to be an astronaut."

"Yes. Absolutely!"

"Well, we would like you to come on board. We will release a formal press notice announcing everyone selected tomorrow at noon. So please don't tell anyone until after that."

"Great. Great. This is great. What do I do?" Huge grin.

"Someone from the astronaut selection office will get in touch with you, and you will get more information. Thanks, Mae. Glad you are joining us."

"Thank you."

I grinned. I sat. I grinned some more. I said to myself, *"Now you've done it." I can't tell anyone. No one? What about my parents? Surely them. Not my sister, she talks too much. God, this is cool. Wow!*

Okay. It's been about 10 minutes, get back to your patient. Don't be all "cheesed up" and everything. Composure. You're a professional.

I settled my face into my "doctor look" and walked back into the examining room. The patient told me about back problems and I began to do a complete physical exam. As I started to look at his pupils, he asked what that had to do with his back. Snapped back to reality, I mumbled something lame like "just a thorough neurological check." I completed the exam and the rest of the day without a hitch.

I went directly from the clinic to my favorite cardio funk aerobics class at Voight Studios with Thea White. I was in high gear. In fact, I felt so great I stayed for a second advanced aerobics class. By the time I arrived back to my apartment I was still pumped. I called my parents, told them, and made them swear not to tell anyone else. (That's how secrecy is lost.) I told Sneeze we were moving to Houston. He was completely okay with it.

I decided the fitting thing to do was to stay up until midnight and watch reruns of *Star Trek*. Afterwards, I finally went to sleep.

The next morning, I woke up with barely time to shower, dress, and look kempt. I jumped into my car and drove the 45 minutes to work. As I was walking out of an examining room that morning my nurse Juan Torres came up to me and said, "You didn't tell us did you Dr. J?"

"Didn't tell you what?"

"That you got accepted to the astronaut program."

"How do you know?"

"Because, there have been 10 phone calls from news stations trying to reach you. The messages are on your desk."

My life had changed. Those messages were a sign that sometimes you can't go back.

ROGER THAT ... EVERYTHING IS LOOKING GOOD

When we first arrived in Houston, the task was to get everyone in my astronaut class of 1987 to a common baseline level of information about human spaceflight. We had test pilots, a meteorologist, an astrophysicist, a mechanical engineer, a medical doctor (me), and a NASA flight controller in our class. We did parachute and survival training, not for use with the space shuttle, but for contingencies with the T-38 super-sonic aircraft astronauts fly in.

That's right, I said supersonic aircraft. Two-seaters. I had flown on a Concorde with a patient in tow and an IV drip running when I was a doctor in West Africa. But suddenly we were talking oxygen masks, helmets, call signs, gauges, and ejection seats. As a mission specialist I was neither expected nor trained to fly the planes on my own, but rather to be a useful crewmember in the backseat: to handle the radios, fly straight and level, follow headings and the flight course, control the plane once off the ground, and plan the flight.

We learned about spacecraft and orbital dynamics. Spacecraft are very different from airplanes and how one navigates an orbit is different from how one navigates an airplane's flight. We learned of the human body's response to weightlessness and the hazards of spaceflight. We learned about the history of human spaceflight, what happened to cause the *Challenger* accident, the innards of the space shuttle, NASA sites, aerospace contractors, and research. Planetology, geology, meteorology. And we learned about one another.

Just before the de-orbit that would bring the *Endeavour* and our crew back to Earth, I perched quietly, looking out of the windows on the flight deck. *Strange, but I always knew I'd be here.*

Looking down and all around me, seeing the Earth, the moon, and the stars, I just felt like I belonged right there, and in fact, any place in the entire universe. And I had known since I was seven years old that the universe was a very big place. Floating up in there in the shuttle, I tried to imagine what it would be like to never travel into space again, to remain forever on Earth. And that felt just fine, which I would never have guessed.

And then I imagined that I was traveling around a star 10,000 light years away and would never return to Earth. And that felt just fine, as well. In fact, I felt so calm that I recognized I would feel comfortable anywhere in the universe—because I belonged to and was a part of it, as much as any star, planet, asteroid, comet, or nebula. Didn't my body and mind contain the same atoms and energy as do the stars?

WHERE THE WIND GOES

The air stirred by the heat of the engines as the Space Shuttle Endeavour roared into the sky not only shook the viewing stands six miles away with a chest rattling rumble, but also my future.

I was not only the first African American woman in space, but also the first woman of color in the world to go into space. The trip brought fame and fanfare: I was named one of *People* Magazine's "Fifty Most Beautiful People in the World" in 1993; won honors and awards such as induction into the National Women's Hall of Fame and the Johnson Publishing Trail Blazer Award; received letters from people around the world; and fielded requests to appear in commercials and to commentate on TV news programs, and even to host television programs. But most significantly my role in the spaceflight provided me a stronger, more visible platform from which to discuss the importance of individuals taking responsibility not only for themselves, but also for how they treat others and this planet.

I resigned from NASA in 1993 and started a technology consulting company to pursue my ideas on integrating social issues into technology design. One of the first projects I started was *The Earth We Share (TEWS)* international science camp, and other programs that arose from my ideas about the most important reasons for science education—critical thinking and problem-solving skills. I began teaching environmental studies at Dartmouth College in Hanover, New Hampshire. As a professor, I was challenged by students to continue my personal and professional growth, and I challenged them to understand the myriad possibilities in the world.

When I left NASA, I left not because I was done with space exploration, but because I wanted to apply my knowledge, skills, perspectives, and energy in innovative ways that the astronaut corps leadership and environment at the time hindered. To be clear, I loved space exploration whether with human travel or not, and I believed in space technology's potential to be a uniquely positive force in the world for everyone. And, while I honestly believed that there was much I could contribute and gain inside NASA, as an astronaut, I had to make a choice — weigh and accept the risks and attendant benefits of remaining at NASA as an astronaut, or, at 36, leave an envied job to find and establish a new destination of my own making.

In 2012, the currents generated by that decision led me to lead 100 Year Starship, an initiative committed to ensuring that the capabilities for human interstellar travel beyond our solar system to another star will exist within the next 100 years. In truth, it was the integration of all the insight gathered from my experiences with projects, travel, people and institutions throughout my life that prompted me to conclude that I knew how "to do" interstellar. The proposal that won a competitive grant from DARPA, built upon key principles I embraced. Everyone should benefit from the bounty of this planet and its resources, not just those already well positioned. Solutions, technologies, and systems are more sustainable and beneficial when they are built drawing upon the full range of human perspective, skills, experiences, and talents. Generally little is accomplished from being timid when big changes are needed—not being injudicious—not just being timid.

An Inclusive Audacious Journey Transforms Life Here on Earth and Beyond was the title of our winning proposal. So despite the fact that I had left the established space program, I still work on the future of space exploration and this work has spawned other projects like *LOOK UP!* which builds on the connection we all feel when we look at the sky.

I have spoken to the United Nations and testified in front of the U.S. Congress. I design projects with engineers, physicians, anthropologists, and entertainers to try to ensure that all people know that they have a place in this world. Each one of us has the right and the responsibility to live up to our individual potential and ambitions.

There are now five other African American women astronauts and more women of color in space. A woman holds the record for the most days in space by any U.S. astronaut and women have commanded both the shuttle and the space station. The Artemis program to return humans to the moon has been announced.

So many things have happened since I left NASA. Many good, and unfortunately a few tragic and sad. I have travelled widely and taken up new causes.

Every now and then, while walking outside in my neighborhood in Houston, or in Tunisia, or the Artic, I feel a slight breeze on my cheek. I look around me. I look up at the sky. Maybe I will see the moon, a star, or the sun. I study my surroundings. Perhaps it's a beautiful flower that captures my eye. A bird. A cat slipping home after a late night out.

I survey my surroundings. I may see derelict buildings or a beautiful palace. I have visited the pyramids again. I saw the Nile from space. Perhaps I may see the John Hancock building towering above me on a Chicago morning. Even as I may be dismayed by the pain, the misery, or the immensity of the problems facing billions of people worldwide, I know beauty is always present. There is hope and direction if we pay attention. The breeze tickles my face, and I know I have unraveled some of its secrets.

Ah, but there stirs another leaf … and I know for the rest of my life I will continue to seek new directions to find where the wind goes.

FOLLOW DR. MAE TODAY

twitter.com/MaeJemison

instagram.com/theRealMaeJemison

www.DrMae.com

SIGNAL HILL ROAD PUBLISHING, LLC

Stories To Elevate and Ideas That Dare

Standing high above the port city of Freetown in Sierra Leone, Signal Hill serves to guide incoming ships and hopeful souls. Signal Hill Road itself twists and turns and provides a beautiful view of city, ocean, and the sprawling continent of Africa. Like our inspirational vista, Signal Hill Road Publishing, LLC serves to provide a unique view of the rapidly evolving worlds of science and social issues through publishing and reaching all ages. We are committed to engaging challenging and unique ideas in ways that broaden our path to the future while improving life here today. We aspire to present world-changing concepts in enthralling and inspirational presentation in both word and image.

SIGNALHILLROAD.COM

Stories To Elevate and Ideas That Dare

9 781637 250006